Praise for
Imagine the Life You'd Love

"I have watched Peg Conley implement the life she imagined. This is a rich buffet of delicious ideas that will nurture your journey toward the life you long to live."

—Mary Anne Radmacher,
author of *SHE* and *Live Boldly*

"*Imagine the Life You'd Love to Live, Then Live It* is a love letter to everyone who has ever had a secret dream. If you know you want to make changes in your life but aren't sure exactly what those changes are or how to do it, Peg Conley offers a cornucopia of practical ideas, suggestions, and questions to inspire and guide you."

—Tina Gilbertson,
author of *Constructive Wallowing*

"Peg Conley is a true inspiration. Her new book, *Imagine the Life You'd Love to Live, Then Live It*, speaks to the dreamer in all of us and provides us with the tools to make our dreams come true. I loved this empowering book because it was clearly written by someone who is really living what she's teaching. Peg's love of life shines through every page and her book can help you in oh-so-many ways. 5 stars!"

—Tony Burroughs,
author of *Get What You Want:
The Art of Making and Manifesting Your Intentions*

"I am a huge fan of Peg Conley's cards, journals, and other gorgeously crafted stationery from Words and Watercolors. Her book is inspiring me to remember to take that all-important 'me time' and do some creative self-care. Her ideas will set your imagination on fire!"

—Reeda Joseph,
author of *Girlfriends Are Lifesavers*

"Through engaging anecdotes and concrete, practical tips, Peg Conley makes it possible for us not only to imagine the life we desire, but to turn our imagined dreams into reality. Conley's approach is accessible, her strategies doable, and by the time you glide through even a couple of these chapters, you'll know how to unlock your own inner genius and you'll be inspired to do it."

—Polly Campbell,
author of *Imperfect Spirituality:*
Extraordinary Enlightenment for Ordinary People

imagine
the life you'd
love to live,
then live it

imagine the life you'd love to live, *then live it*

52 inspired habits and playful prompts

by Peg Conley

Foreword by Reverend Maggie Oman Shannon

VIVA
EDITIONS

ONONDAGA FREE

Published in the United States by Viva Editions, an imprint of
Cleis Press, Inc., 2246 Sixth Street, Berkeley, California 94710.

Printed in the United States.
Cover design: Scott Idleman/Blink
Cover art: Peg Conley
Text design: Frank Wiedemann

First Edition.
10 9 8 7 6 5 4 3 2 1

Trade paper ISBN: 978-1-936740-87-1
E-book ISBN: 978-1-63228-01-5

Library of Congress Cataloging-in-Publication Data is available.

TABLE OF CONTENTS

foreword

If you're reading these words, chances are you picked up *Imagine the Life You'd Love to Live, Then Live It* because you're looking for some ideas, some inspiration, something that will support you either in taking a step toward your dreams or in fully living the life of your dreams. I've got good news for you: This wise little book fits that bill nicely!

So often we tell ourselves—even if we know better—that getting to the life of our dreams is a smooth trajectory, a pole-vault leap from Point A to Point B, that will happen once _____ (fill in the blank). And as a Unity minister who regularly teaches the spiritual principle of Law of Mind Action, popularly known as the Law of Attraction, I see this tendency to believe that by making our vision board and saying our affirmations and visualizing really, really hard, that our dream-life will just magically, and suddenly, manifest. And certainly, vision boards and affirmations and visualizations have their place—in fact, you will be reading about them in these pages. But we need to remember that we only have one day at a time, and that dreams are built one step at a time. Chances are pretty good that we're not going to move from Point A to Point B on any given day...but we can take actions today that will move the ball down the playing field of our lives—until one day, we will wake up, and indeed find that we are living that dream we have long held

xi

in our minds and hearts (and which is often even better than what we imagined)!

That's the key, and why this book is so helpful...because its message is to use each day to move the ball forward, even if it's just a smidgen; in other words, this book teaches us to choose to see each day as sacred, as the dough from which our piece of the pie is crafted. That's how dream-lives are created...living mindfully and intentionally, one day at a time. Happily for all of us, Peg gives plenty of ideas for how to live lives that inspire others and ourselves, speaking as a dear friend would with words of encouragement and grace. "You don't have to completely make over your entire life to see change," Peg writes. "It can be as easy as cleaning your closets." And not only do we not have to tackle all closets in one day (or whatever your big project is), Peg invites us to perhaps take a few Saturdays in a row to get it done. Kind advice, common-sense advice—and the kind of advice that can indeed move our lives from Point A to Point B.

Small steps and inspired ideas including the ones you will find within these pages can eventually yield great rewards...but perhaps even more importantly, they can bless the experience of each of our days with "magic and miracles...serendipities and synchronicities." As Peg promises and so supportively and convincingly demonstrates, it really is that simple.

Reverend Maggie Oman Shannon
Unity minister and author of *Crafting Calm*

"We're going to move there!" was Carole's reply to my question of how was their trip to New Zealand. She and Scott, her husband, had looked forward to visiting that land of adventure for years. Scott has been working at various wineries in the Livermore Valley of California and wanted to experience, first-hand, how things were done in the wineries of New Zealand. Closing in on retirement from the military, Scott had begun taking classes in viticulture and enology three years previously at the local community college. He was still working with the military, but spent most nights and weekends in the wine world. He even bottled his own vintage in 2013, a Cabernet that he began in 2011 with the crush followed by barrel aging.

I'd gotten to know Carole as a buyer for a nursery in the Bay Area. She had been buying my greeting cards for the store, and from the moment I met her, I was reminded of one of my best friends from college. Needless to say, we hit it off and always enjoyed chatting with each other. I was very excited to hear that they finally fulfilled their long-held dream of vacationing in New Zealand—a dream come true. And Scott was even offered a job with a winery down there. They had often talked of having a B&B in the wine country of the Livermore Valley, but with the price of real estate, that dream was prohibitive. This opportunity in New Zealand offered not only a chance for Scott to learn winemaking at the hands of master vintners but allowed the dream of a B&B to seem possible. Carole, with her degree and background in horticulture, would be able to learn about the flora and fauna of a different but similar climate and possibly turn her own dream into a reality. From an outsider's position, it all appeared quite effortless.

They headed to New Zealand in the spring, just in time for the busy fall season for grapes in the southern hemisphere.

And that, dear friend, is my hope for you in reading this book: that you can imagine the life you want to live and then live it, ever so simply! Carole and Scott's story has all the components of living the imagined life. They visualized, dreamed, planned, and prepared. They believed, took action, and contacted people. It's not as easy as snapping your fingers, but it is similar to "if you build it they will come." You've got to believe it, build it (take action steps), and keep moving forward—trusting that the dream will unfold in countless, creative ways that even you can't begin to imagine.

The ideas in this book are all tried-and-true exercises that I've done at one time or another. You'll read my stories of change and transformation as I, oh-so-hesitantly at times, moved in the direction of my dreams. Granted, it can be downright scary to launch yourself into the unknown, but it is also exhilarating to realize that you are doing exactly what it is you have always wanted to do.

I'm a dreamer. I've dreamed up lots of interesting experiences in my life, from traveling around Europe with a Eurail pass, to moving out West over 30 years ago, not to mention imagining this creative life I'm now living. Life has provided many wonderful adventures along the way. They don't always unfold exactly the way I envision, but the essence is always there and often it is far better than I ever imagined.

I hope this book inspires you to develop some new habits and disciplines that will lead to creating the well-imagined life for yourselves. I'd love to hear about the surprises and the magic that happens along the way!

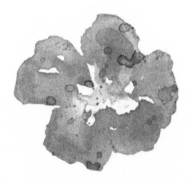

chapter one

Imagine

When I first "heard" these words, I thought to myself, I must be crazy: *Imagine the life you want to live... then live it! (It's that simple).* Immediately I asked myself, who can actually do whatever it is they want to do? And how can it be that simple? It's not unusual for me to "hear" words that come into my consciousness. I often get the words to pair with the watercolor images I create. But that statement seemed like a stretch, even for me. I was preparing my submissions for my 2011 "In the Garden" calendar that Brush Dance published each year. It was the spring of 2009 and I had just relocated to San Francisco from Seattle. I was in the midst of a *huge* transition in my life and my feet were not yet planted on firm soil. Leaving Seattle meant leaving 25 years of corporate sales in addition to my (now adult) children, my beloved home, and many friends. The trade-off: I was recently married and my new husband had moved from San Francisco to join me in Seattle. (We had been friends in high school in Indiana, but that's another story.) Mark wanted to return to San Francisco and enticed me with the suggestion that I could do my art if I relocated to California. I remember being so excited at the thought of "living the creative life," as I called it, that I could barely sleep the night after we had the first of many discussions.

Many of my friends and certainly my children questioned why I would move to California. Why would I give up my home (which I loved), my job (which I loved) and a life (which I loved)? Only to move to a city where I didn't know anyone save my husband? Besides that, it was the fall of 2008 and the world seemed to quickly be going to hell in a handbasket. Initially we planned that I would find a job in my field and then someday I'd quit and begin the creative life I'd been imagining (for years). But things never quite go as planned—because of the economy I didn't find that great sales position that would have kept me gainfully employed, with money deposited in my checking account every two weeks. Instead, I found a job that was frustrating on many levels. Less than six months later, I quit. Mark had suggested, after my house sold, that I take the money and do what I always wanted to do—make a living from my artwork. I stumbled for a good while, clearly in the larva/cocoon stage of metamorphosis: not sure how I was going to transform myself from corporate sales queen to self-supporting artist.

I had made the jump off the cliff and was still floating down to the shelf below, not sure how or where I was going to land. It was about this time that I "heard" the words that became the title of this book. The advice, out of nowhere, resonated at a profound level.

Four years later, I can easily make a case for how "It's that simple" can work. Then, I had no clue that I'd resurrect the name of a greeting card line that I began 15 years earlier, and launch myself on a creative path that would include starting my own greeting card company, as well as licensing my art with other manufacturers. But that is just what happened.

I won't say it was easy or effortless, but with the help of my imagination, countless entries in my journal, brainstorming sessions with myself and a newsprint pad, creating vision boards, writing and repeating goals and affirmations—not to mention the support from my husband and my new friends in San Francisco—I've done it! I've created the Imagined Life.

What do you imagine your ideal life to be? It may take some time for it to unveil itself. You will need to have an idea of what it is you are looking to create. Spend some time in contemplation. For some, that means a quiet meditation where images might come to you. For others, you might write about something you've always had a longing to create, or a dream that seemed far away and unattainable yet doesn't go away. The dream nudges at you, asking you to pay attention. Where words work for some people, pictures work for others. You may want to create a vision board. Gather your old magazines and begin ripping out the pictures that appeal to you. Your Ideal Life will come alive via the images that resonate with you, or you can draw your own images. Don't hesitate to pick up a pen, pencil, or crayons, even, and fill the blank pages with doodles of any kind. Do you still think of becoming a nurse? Don't be disheartened; go online and research classes you can take at your local college to start the process. As someone told me once, if you don't start now, five years from now you still will be where you are. But if you begin with baby steps, in five years you could be in a completely different place!

- So ask yourself the question: What does the life I long to live look like?
- Imagine it. Draw it, write it, collage it, and just plain dream it.

Believe you can have it, and then go about creating it as you daily take steps toward becoming an enhanced version of yourself.

All successful people, men and women, are big dreamers. They imagine what their future could be, ideal in every respect, and then they work every day toward their distant vision, that goal or purpose.

—BRIAN TRACY,
Universal Laws of Success

chapter two

Take a Class

had an idea for a book but knew I needed some help with the craft of writing. (I didn't think the boxes of journals in my basement would count for much experience.) I took a nonfiction writing class at the San Francisco Writer's Grotto. Not only did I learn skills from a professional, I met Lauren, who would become one of my trusted and true friends. And I met Steve, a gifted and talented writer, whom I would seek out for valuable and informative advice on various writing projects.

It had been a long time since I'd been in a classroom and had actual weekly assignments to complete when I took the eight-week class at the Grotto that fall. But I found myself energized by the camaraderie of the class, the reading and writing homework, and the things we were learning. I had never considered submitting my writing to a magazine, and yet, after that class, I actually looked at the editorial page of a magazine, as we were taught, searching out the information needed for a submittal. I did submit ideas to a few magazines and did the follow-up. My work wasn't accepted, but I did have encouraging conversations with people at the various magazines that I contacted. I had been impressed with the fact that Ethan Watters, our teacher, actually made his living as a writer. He was one of the original founders of the Writer's Grotto, not to mention a contributor to numerous magazines: *New York Times*, *GQ*, *Esquire,* and many others, and he had completed two books as well. I tried to implement what I had learned even in my journal entries. Ethan encouraged us to be descriptive and detailed in our writing. I likened the process to painting a picture. I'd start out with a rough sketch, which was the rough draft, and then home in on what worked and throw out what didn't. I realized he was correct in saying that the more detailed and descriptive the writing, the better the story, as the reader could "see" the details clearly in their mind's eye.

After the class ended, a core group of us continued meeting every two weeks. Ethan had suggested that developing an ongoing writers group would provide the support and encouragement needed to continue to hone our respective writing skills. He was correct. We continued to write, read, and critique each other's work for at least six months. Then the busyness of life took its toll and schedule conflicts continued until we stopped meeting.

From a teaching perspective, I've taught a number of watercolor workshops. It is so rewarding to watch people overcome their inner critic, as they learn that they can "play" with watercolors instead of believing that they need to create a masterpiece each time they pick up a pencil or brush. Recently I had a woman tell me that she hadn't done any art since she was in grade school and was admonished for not being "good" at art. If I could go back in time, I would have a serious conversation with that teacher about the negative impact her comment would have on her student for decades. Thankfully, that day the woman broke through her belief that she was unable to create art. Instead she proudly held her painting high, describing how she felt about the process and what she learned during the show-and-tell portion of the class.

- What interests you?
- What subject would you like to become proficient in?
- What skills do you want to acquire?
- What's your passion?

Find a class and explore and expand your skill set, knowledge base, and view of yourself. San Francisco State University has a College of Extended Learning, which offers hundreds of classes for professional development and personal enrichment. What does your local college offer? Make a list of classes that interest you and register for one. You can also find classes at your local community center, church, library—or even where you shop for yarn (knitting classes), or fabric (quilting classes), or the gym (yoga classes).

> Be open to learning new skills,
> meeting new people, and having F-U-N!
> I live for Pilates reformer class. I go at least three times a
> week. It's a great way to lengthen your muscles, stretch,
> and kind of relax your mind.
>
> —SHAWN JOHNSON,
> 2008 Olympic gold medal gymnast

chapter three

Write with Your Nondominant Hand

You'll be amazed at the wisdom that pours forth. Joni, a therapist I worked with, introduced me to this concept many years ago. She was a big proponent of working with your "inner child" to achieve healing. Upon her recommendation, I purchased a book titled *Recovery of Your Inner Child*, with the subtitle "The Highly Acclaimed Method for Liberating Your Inner Self," written by Lucia Capacchione, PhD. Through exercises in the book, I was able to reconnect with "Peggy," my own inner child. I had made such a big deal about wanting to be called "Peg" when I went off to college that I hadn't been called "Peggy" in probably 20 years when I began this process. I remember being shocked when I drew a picture of Peggy, complete with her glasses and curly hair. She was so cute! She was playful and clearly opened me up to the idea that magic was all around us. I honestly believe that "Peggy" was able to feel, finally, that I was going to pay attention and listen to her, as I completed the various exercises in that book. At first it felt awkward to hold a pen in my left hand, not to mention my penmanship, which looked like that of a seven-year-old.

From my own experience, I can see that being open to the magic surrounding "Peggy" helped me unleash my inner artist and opened me to the idea that I could, indeed, one day "live the creative life," as I now call it. When I began writing with my nondominant hand, I began to realize that I was drawing on wisdom that was universal. I would begin writing by addressing "Peggy" with my right hand and writing a question. Then when ready for the answer, I would shift the pen to my left hand. In switching the pen (or pencil) from the right hand to left, you access a different part of your brain, the left side of the brain governs the analytical while the right side governs the artistic. I stopped addressing "Peggy" after a while and instead would address my guides, angels, ancestors, or whatever sounded right at the time.

One day, while struggling with a recurring issue, I grabbed my journal and instead of merely recording my frustrations, I began by addressing my guides and asking for help/insight with the situation at hand. I could feel something shift as I switched the pen from my right hand to my left. The words that poured forth comforted me: "Surrender to the Moon, the Sky, the Stars... Peace results... Rest in the comfort of the invisible hands that hold and guide... The Hidden World supports us!" Those words allowed me to relax and remember the power of "letting go and letting God." I put those words on one of my greeting cards, paired with an image of the moon.

I believe we are able to find our authentic selves when we cut through the personalities we wear like masks to conceal who we really are from others as well as ourselves.

Over the years, I have used this technique often, and then long periods of time will pass when I don't write at all with my nondominant hand. Something will trigger me to try it again, and I'll marvel at the insights I receive and pledge to be more consistent with the practice. Just yesterday I was writing about a situation, and the appropriate answer, which my personality-self and dominant hand clearly would have missed, was to think of this world as a playground rather than a school. When the world is a playground, it can be playful and fun. When it's a school, I need to learn lessons, pay attention, do the right thing. I totally loved the idea of thinking of myself as being on a playground, and will try to keep that front and center in my awareness as I go about daily life.

- Address your guides, angels, or whoever you call on as you write with your dominant hand, explaining the question or issue that you have. Then, as you switch hands, become aware of any shift in yourself.
- Sit quietly for a few minutes and then begin writing.
- Try writing like this over a period of time. Whenever you are confronted with a baffling issue, turn to your own inner wisdom for guidance.

Don't fret about the difficulty of writing this way. You are accessing a different part of your brain—your wisdom—even though the writing might look like a second-grader's! Do it often. You'll be amazed at all the answers that lie within.

> The right side of the brain, which controls the left hand, will say things you don't know that you know. It specializes in assessing your physical and mental feelings, and it often offers solutions. "Take a nap," your right hemisphere might say, or "Just do what feels right; we'll be fine." You'll find there's a little Zen master in that left hand of yours.
>
> —MARTHA BECK,
> *Finding Your Own North Star*

chapter four

Meditate

You've heard the advice a million times: Meditate as a path to enlightenment and discovery about yourself. It calms you down. Brings you back to your center. Provides insight. Why would you not want to try it? All major religions advocate some sort of mindfulness prayer or quiet time.

The benefits are amazing. They range from the physiological to the psychological to the spiritual. Studies show that 15–20 minutes of meditation per day are all you need to attain many benefits. A few of the physiological benefits are an increase in blood flow, lower heart rate, and lower risk of cardiovascular disease; meditation harmonizes our endocrine system and relaxes our nervous system. Psychological benefits include increased creativity, increased feelings of vitality and rejuvenation, slower aging of the mind, an ability to see the larger picture in a given situation, and a decreased tendency to worry. That last one alone makes it worthwhile! Our spiritual nature is improved through meditation, as we are able to keep things in perspective. It brings body, mind, and spirit into harmony, helps us learn to live in the present moment, and can increase both intuition and the synchronicity in your life.

There are so many ways to meditate. You can try breathing meditations, walking meditations, listening to a guided meditation. I've tried numerous types of meditations; one of my favorites is a kind of drawing meditation. You can enter into another zone as you concentrate on the drawing at hand. The outside world drops away as I enter that zone of concentration, when looking at a subject to sketch and then sketching. As I merge with the task at hand, I find I go on automatic pilot, almost, as the drawing seems to complete itself. I never fail to be surprised at the end result. When I first look at a sketch or painting I've completed while "in the zone," I'm typically surprised and shocked—because clearly the work is inspired by a higher version of myself. Try it!

There are so many ways to learn how to meditate. You can take a class, read a book, try a guided CD, or find any number of offerings on the Internet, from Zen Buddhist meditation to Mindfulness Meditation to Transcendental Meditation. I found that if I get up early I can sit for 15 minutes easily by myself. It is such a grounding way to begin the day. You can almost get out in front of your day by sitting quietly and envisioning that all will go well throughout the day.

I do my morning meditation upon awakening. I've found if I don't do it then, it doesn't get done—the busy day begins to fill in the minutes and hours. I begin by slowly repeating, "I breathe deeply... And completely..." Over and over I repeat the phrase, inhaling slowly as I say, "I breathe deeply," holding the breath a few seconds and then slowly exhaling as I say, "and completely." I was taught this relaxation technique in my first experience with meditation many years ago. I was always so surprised at how the meditation practice could quiet my rapid, firecracker mind, allowing me to truly relax and enter a different level of consciousness.

After breathing deeply and completely, I open my crown chakra (at the top of my head) and envision connecting with a beam of light that is directly from the Source, or Heaven or Divine Light or Father Sky, whatever I happen to call it that day. After I feel that connection is made, I open my root chakra (at the base of my spine) and envision connecting with Mother Earth, or Nature, to allow this rod of light to go up and down along my spine as I ask it to guide me as I move about the day. I also envision my heart being open and sending out rays of golden energy to the world. Monkey mind, which is a Buddhist term for the unsettled, restless, and capricious mind that clamors for attention like a bunch of drunken monkeys, often sets in after I begin the practice. Rather than banishing the monkeys, I learned to keep breathing slowly and completely and to focus on the breath, while at the same time acknowledging their existence. My mind often wants to race ahead—to create an agenda for the day or to contemplate conversations or to imagine the worst that can happen in a given situation. Returning to the breath, I focus on the inhale and then the exhale, and slowly the monkeys take flight. Then I'm left with the peace and serenity that meditation offers.

- Consider a practice of meditation. Sit quietly for just five minutes a day to begin. You can increase the time as you choose.

- Listen to a guided meditation. Any number of resources are available on the Internet.

Meditation is not a way of making your mind quiet. It's a way of entering into the quiet that's already there— buried under the 50,000 thoughts the average person thinks every day.

—DEEPAK CHOPRA,
The Seven Spiritual Laws of Success

chapter five

Let Your Heart
Lead You

T hose words came to me shortly after I moved to San Francisco. What I didn't know when I first encountered the thought was that I would be continually challenged to lead my life from the heart, not the head. This was not an easy concept for me to grasp. I had years of practice in "figuring things out" and trusting my head over my heart. It sounded rather willy-nilly to live from the heart as opposed to the head. How does one even do that? It's been four and a half years and I'm still learning. Even though I've had amazing experiences when I have listened to my heart and acted on what I hear or feel or intuit, I'm still inclined to doubt myself and go to my head for advice.

Here's how the story of learning to listen to my heart came to pass: Shortly after relocating to San Francisco, I was on a plane headed to Atlanta. After disembarking, I was approaching baggage claim when I heard someone ask, "Which carousel?" "San Francisco, #7" came the reply. I then realized that I was now living in the city of St. Francis. I flashed on my favorite prayer, "Make Me a Channel of Your Peace," the prayer of St. Francis. I lived in Seattle for 20 years—a city named after Chief Sealth. While living there I learned of Native American ways and studied to become a shaman. I wondered what I'd learn now that I was living in the City of St. Francis.

A few weeks later, I was on a plane again, this time traveling back to San Francisco from Seattle. On the plane I had begun to read Sonia Choquette's book, *The Answer is Simple...Love Yourself, Live Your Spirit,* a gift from my daughter, Emily. Sonia's book about letting go of Ego and living from Spirit showed me that it's another way of saying letting go of Mind/Intellect and living from the Heart. I closed my eyes to think about it, and here's what came up.

My stone St. Francis statue used to grace the patio of my house in Seattle, but it was relegated to the top of the stairs in the entry of our new (old Victorian) apartment in San Francisco. A week before, I had heard a bong, kerplunk, kerplunk, bang, bong... I couldn't imagine what had happened to cause such a racket. I discovered that the kitties, chasing their little ball, had knocked St. Francis down the stairwell. To my horror, I realized he had been decapitated! I picked up his head and wondered, What the heck? In my shaman world, I had been taught to look at everything that happens as a metaphor. If you look beyond the face value of situations and circumstances, you can sometimes find answers in the most unlikely places. It took me a few days to contemplate the meaning of St. Francis losing his head, and then, reading Sonia's book, it came to me so clearly! What a perfect metaphor for allowing the mind/intellect to roll down the stairs. It was time for the heart/soul to have a voice. What I didn't realize at the time was the power of metamorphosis. I was in the cocoon of change; this insight would allow me to view things from a completely different perspective. Living in the city of St. Francis was going to be interesting. There is a lot of heart in San Francisco.

- How does your heart see things?
- What path would it lead you down? (Likely a much different path than the one your head would like you to travel.)

- Sit with this thought for a few moments (or days), and then journal about any ideas that pop into your head.

I believe the heart whispers, while the head isn't shy about yelling its demands. You may need time to practice "hearing" your heart. Listen to conversations with close friends and family. Your heart reveals itself in many different ways. Sometimes you'll hear a song that holds meaning for you, or you'll see a billboard with a message. A book will open to the page that holds answers you were seeking. The heart can be subtle, but it is oh, so powerful. Give it voice and you'll never be disappointed.

> The most beautiful things in the world cannot be seen or even touched, they must be felt with the heart.
>
> —HELEN KELLER

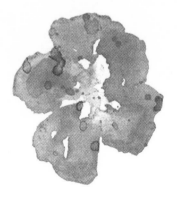

chapter six

Get Nurtured in Nature

Go outside! Play in your garden. Dig in the dirt. Look up at the sky. See shapes in the clouds. Touch the bark of the trees as you walk past. Inhale the fragrance of the pines. Take off your shoes and delight in wiggling your toes in the cool green grass or the hard-packed sand at the water's edge. Listen to the birds chirping. Feel the sun on your face, the wind in your hair. As you connect with nature, you will find your stress level lowered, your anxiety calmed, and your mood lifted. Spending time in the great outdoors can also sharpen your mental capabilities and enhance your creativity.

I have long known about the incredible benefits of being in nature. As young kids we could play for hours outdoors. Some of my fondest memories as a child are of being outside playing. Whether it was jumping in the big piles of leaves we'd rake each fall as the old oak trees shed their colorful leaves, or building forts made of snow from a winter's storm, or running races on the gravel driveway barefoot in the summer, I always felt so happy and completely in the moment when outside. What are some of your favorite memories of playing outdoors as a child? Do you still do it?

My love of nature has been with me all my adult life. I've never been one to go to a gym for a workout, instead preferring any kind of activity that takes me outdoors. From running to hiking, biking, and walking, just being outdoors is not only exercise for my body but also nurturing for my soul.

Nature reminds us of the Divine. Mother Nature is so much bigger than us. She's the ocean, the night sky studded with stars, the fragrant whiff of jasmine. I pay homage to her as I embrace her tree trunks, dip my toes in the cold ocean water, and feel the sun on my face.

In college I learned the benefits of spending time outdoors. When stuck on a design project or unable to solve a problem, I'd go out for a run. As many people have experienced, the answer comes effortlessly when we let go of the worry and intense focus on the problem and instead shift to being in the moment. The wind in our hair, the sweat on our brow, the smell of cut grass as we run by—all serve to focus us on the here and now. And suddenly the answer pops into our head; the solution to a problem; the idea to call someone. Peace and serenity follow.

Even today, when I get stressed out, I know it is time to lace up my walking shoes and head out the door for a quick walk or drive to one of my favorite parks for a brisk hike.

When I lived in Seattle and ran a lot, I discovered a street that led down to the beach. It was a normal street, with homes on both sides, and then abruptly the homes gave way to trees and underbrush. Suddenly you entered a magical grove where the fairies lived! I loved running down the hill, which was forested heavily for probably about a quarter of a mile. When I would do that run, I'd ask for the fairies to fill me with their special "gold and silver sprinkle dust," so I'd have enough of it to sprinkle on whoever I would come in contact with who needed some magic.

I developed the habit of touching trees while my daughter, Emily, and I hiked along trails when she was young. We'd shout out the names of the qualities we thought the trees embodied and what they shared with us as we touched them: "Grace," "Gentleness," "Strength," "Compassion." It was a fun game. We'd note the various sizes of the trunks, the moss growing on the trees, and the different textures of bark. To this day, I still touch the bark of the trees as I walk along—it is my way of literally getting in touch with nature.

- What do you do to get in touch with nature? Have you ever considered the notion that nature can nurture?

- Spend some time in nature and record your observations, be it a sketch or thoughts you had as you walked along.

- Did you see any magical dragonflies along the way?

> Look deep into nature, and then you will understand everything better.
>
> —ALBERT EINSTEIN

chapter seven

Play...Create...Explore!

Those words came to me as I was contemplating a title for a calendar idea I was developing. I wanted to encourage, in monthly segments, various projects or ideas that people could develop and build on that would allow for creativity to be explored. I had already discovered, from teaching watercolor workshops, that when I suggested people take the attitude of "playing" with their art, they would naturally loosen up and not be so critical with themselves about their lack of ability, "not being good enough," or whatever it is that held them back from the free-flowing play of exploration.

Actually, the idea was the genesis of this book. I was so excited as I scribbled my ideas for the suggestions for each month into my notebook—it was as if the top of my head had lifted off and the inspiration was pouring forth. I couldn't write fast enough to capture all the ideas that were filing in. Creativity at its finest: it was flowing from my head to my pen. I'd write down a month and then multiple examples of what could be done that month—for example, February: write a love letter each week. I was very spirited as I explained the process of "play, create, explore" to the publisher to whom I was pitching my calendar. Then a few weeks later I was telling a friend about the entire experience, including my excitement when pitching the idea. My friend, Maggie Oman Shannon, had just wrapped up the writing of her book, *Crafting Calm,* with a publisher, Viva Editions, and she suggested I contact the publisher myself and pitch a book idea. "Really!?" I asked. Still with a playful heart, and creativity jumping in arcs around me, I crafted an email to Brenda Knight— and the rest, as they say, is herstory!

Just as I had experienced the power of my own explorations into playful creativity, I knew that if I could engage the childlike wonder that comes with play, creativity would flourish for others as well. That's what I wanted to continue to explore: the playful process of creativity rather than the labored fixating on an end result. And that's what it's all about. (You do the hokey pokey and you turn yourself around. "That's what it's all about!") It's being in the moment as you are creating. You lose yourself in time as you focus your awareness on the activity at hand. I continually surprise myself with the finished piece of art when I'm "in the flow." When I look up and realize an hour has passed, I'm often amazed. Where did the time go?

It's fun to play! Purchase some Crayola crayons—remember that yummy smell when you'd first open a box as a kid? And check out those colors. I always loved reading their descriptive names: mulberry, cornflower, olive green, carnation pink. Explore watercolor pencils or even finger paints, anything to encourage your playful nature. Grab markers and a large newsprint pad of paper. Draw, doodle, write a poem, have fun. Play! As you create, you'll be exploring your creative nature and you'll be impressed with what comes through on the paper. I've seen it happen time and time again when someone holds up their paper at the "show and tell" part of my class and describes with awe the fun they had playing rather than worrying about trying to finish with a perfect sketch or drawing or painting. The best part of all is how impressed they are with the final result.

Almost all creativity involves purposeful play.

—ABRAHAM MASLOW,
one of the founders of Humanistic Psychology

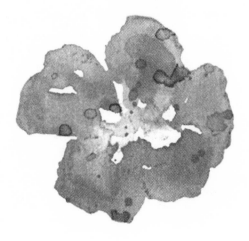

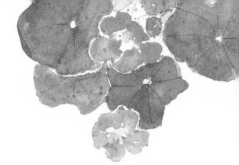

chapter eight

Be Flexible

When I read the words "Be flexible," I think of Gumby, that funny-looking, nearly two-dimensional, green, clay humanoid character who was the star of TV and screen for decades. Gumby can bend and flex at any point in his body; he can be twisted and turned in any direction. (Of course, he's made of clay.) If only we had that range of motion.

The "Be flexible" directive is meant to encourage flexibility in body, mind, and everyday life. If you can be flexible, you can bend and sway with whatever gales and storms blow your way. Even tall skyscrapers are built with inherent flexibility so they can rock and roll with any earthquakes that may occur.

Being able to touch your toes indicates a certain amount of flexibility, as does being able to practice yoga, which over time will increase your chances of touching your toes! Start off your day with some gentle stretches. When you are sitting at your desk and struggling with a problem, take a few moments to stretch, move your head from side to side, stand up, and jiggle your body. Get loose and play like Gumby. Just the movement of your body could dislodge the stuck part of your mind. Before you know it, an answer might appear in your head, or suddenly you'll see what you need to do next to solve the problem. It's uncanny the way our mind and body are linked.

Have an open mind. You can bend and flow with ease when

you keep an open mind. An open mind allows you to accept other people for who they are; it allows you to be curious about the process and not be fixated on any specific outcome. An open mind encourages brainstorming, where you can shout out seemingly ridiculous ideas and nothing is rejected. Being flexible allows for accepting differing points of view. I've always loved and often quoted the phrase "There is no good or bad or right or wrong, there just is." That is what an open mind allows for: no judgment, no "It has to be this way, not that," no telling it like it is—just a simple acceptance to the *all* of life.

Being flexible in everyday life means we flow downstream with the river and let go of disappointment when life doesn't hand us what we want. Being flexible allows for peace of mind, serenity, and being present when things don't go your way—and as we all know, life does not always go the way we think it should! As much as we think we may have all the answers and know what path we are on, thinking we are clear in our goals—something will come along and turn us upside down. That's where learning to be flexible is paramount to a peaceful way of existence.

- When you begin to feel tension in your body, think of yourself as Gumby and flex your body as if it's made of clay.

- Be of flexible mind and body at all times. Notice how much better you feel.

- Try performing a few gentle stretching exercises each morning to increase your flexibility and help set the tone for an easy day.

I don't think of myself as unbreakable. Perhaps I'm just rather flexible and adaptable.

—AUNG SAN SUU KYI,
Burmese politician

chapter nine

Go with the Flow

T he best-laid plans can go awry. When that happens, rather than lament or get upset, I've learned to go with the flow. Ironically, I've also found that if I wait awhile and then revisit the situation, I can see there was a surprise hidden in the disruption. It can turn out to be a blessing in disguise.

What do you think of when you hear "Go with the flow"? To me, it's a reminder to go along with the flow of life. To float with the current, which really is so much easier than trying to swim upstream or across the current. There is nothing more idyllic than spending an afternoon letting the current of a river carry you downstream. Growing up in Indiana, I had the pleasure of spending hot, lazy summer days on Wildcat Creek with my friends. We'd either be floating down the creek in inner tubes or paddling in canoes. Looking back, I had no idea what life lessons I was learning, as we floated effortlessly with the current, splashing in the water, reveling in the summer sun filtering through the canopy of leaves overhead, with the large trees banked on either side. Every once in a while a bit of rapids would cause us to speed up, and then we'd fall back to our relaxed pace. We'd float along knowing that at some point we'd come up to a sandbar, the perfect place to get out for a spell, then back in again to continue our dance with the water, letting it carry us along. That is the essence of going with the flow. No stress, no effort, no forcing, just relaxing into the moment, being carried effortlessly down-stream, stopping to play for a while on the rocks and sand, then scrambling back into the canoe, once again drifting downstream.

Taking that notion and applying it to daily life could make life a whole lot easier. If only we could remember to apply the principle when we need it. I've learned, over the years, that life continues to offer up changes and challenges that disrupt our worldview or our peace of mind. God only knows that our spouses, kids, coworkers, and others don't always act in the manner we'd want them to act, nor do they think the way we think they should. Rather than getting our panties in a bunch, we can extend to them the same acceptance for who they are that we'd like to be accorded. We can just decide to go with the flow and see what happens rather than try to force them to change how they see the world. (Because, as we also know, that rarely happens.) Instead, by surrendering to the situation and allowing the answers to naturally fall in place, we'll often be surprised at how easy life seems to be.

And if you think about it, a simple little song from childhood sums it all up quite nicely.

- Sing along. Loudly and with laughter as you remember it's all a dream!

  Row, row, row your boat,
  Gently down the stream.
  Merrily, merrily, merrily, merrily,
  Life is but a dream!

- Decide to go with the flow and look for the surprise hidden in situations that may challenge you.

Water flows because it's willing.

—MARTY RUBIN,
philosopher

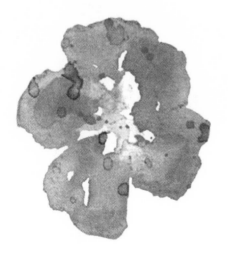

chapter ten

Unplug to Recharge

1 t sounds rather refreshing to unplug and recharge! I've found that it works, too. Though it's certainly fun to see what all your Facebook friends are up to each day, you can post, tweet, read links, and watch endless YouTube videos, and before you know it, hours have passed. You're tired. You are not inspired. And you find it easier to retire, your battery depleted, rather than do something creative, constructive, or fun. Have you ever said this to your kids? "When I was your age, we were outside playing kick the can and hide-and-go-seek. We didn't sit inside and play video games, we were out climbing trees!" Well, take some of your own advice and turn off the technology. Turn off the phone, shut down the computer, and you'll be surprised at how reenergized you'll feel.

What did you do before technology overtook your life? Honor a Sabbath of your own making. It could be Friday night or Sunday morning; you'll find that unplugging allows you to revert to a simpler time. Engage the whole family and plan activities that bring you together. Instead of having each person focused on a computer screen or a smartphone, take turns talking about what animals you see in the clouds while lying in the grass in the backyard, or simply enjoy the bonding that happens as you make breakfast together (pancakes or waffles?) or discuss plans for the weekend (the zoo or beach?). Enjoy the conversation with others rather than individual isolation.

I knew I was on to something when I received my July/August *Fast Company* magazine in the mail. On the cover, in big bold letters, was the headline "#Unplug," with the subtitle, "My life was crazy. So I disconnected for 25 days. You should too." Baratunde Thurston's smiling face beams from the cover as the sidebar notes: "What happens when the world's most connected man takes a digital vacation?" I couldn't wait to read the article. And I was not at all surprised to discover that his observations confirmed what I had intuitively felt: technology is preventing us from making real and heartfelt connections with those close to us—family and friends in our immediate circle, right here, right now.

There were accompanying checklists, quizzes, and how-tos covering subjects from "How to disappear: a nine-point digital detox checklist" to "Are you a digital addict?" and "How the busiest connectors give themselves a break." All good advice to consume and consider as one contemplates just how you can unplug and uncover a different way of life.

The article lists the reasons behind Thurston's recognition that he desperately needed to take a break from constant connectivity. The volume of Facebook postings, Twitter tweets, and Foursquare check-ins was astounding. As he noted, his daily routine and lifestyle had become unsustainable. This was a man who was so plugged in because of his multiple professional roles: author, consultant, CEO, speechwriter/speaker. Working 24/7 was the norm. Once he committed to unplugging, he set about doing the prep work needed to make it happen. There were people to notify, decisions to make about what he would unplug from, and how, and when it would happen. The digital detox was to happen over the holidays; naturally a slowed pace of life during that timeframe helped. From 5:00 p.m. on Friday, December 14th, 2012, through Monday, January 7th, 2013, he

would embrace real world interaction by strengthening relationships with pre-Facebook pals.

What I found most interesting in the article was his reporting
on how the digital detox impacted him. "By the end of that first
week, the quiet rhythm of my days seemed far less strange. I was
less stressed about not knowing new things." I could almost sense
his joy as he reported, "I was reading long books, engaging in
meaningful conversations, and allowing my mind to wander and
make passive connections I had previously short-circuited with
social queries, responses, interruptions, and steady documenting
and sharing of unripened experiences." As one would expect,
when he returned to the land of the digital after experiencing
the gift of restored appreciation for disengagement, silence, and
emptiness, he didn't return at the same crazed level as before.

- What can you do to discover the joys of discon-
  necting?
- Would you consider doing a digital detox? For how
  long? One day a week?

With your newfound time on your hands, plan different activities:

- Put on music that makes you move and dance the
  night (or 15 minutes) away.
- Go to lunch with a friend and catch up in real time
  (rather than Facebook time)
- Make a big pot of soup and invite your neighbors
  over for Sunday dinner.

I have those moments with my kids and family where we try to unplug and just be in the moment. We put everything else to the side and just be there with our family.

—SOLEIL MOON FRYE,
actress/director/screenwriter

chapter eleven

Look for Magic and Miracles

One thing I've noticed is that if I put myself on alert, so to speak, I'll "see" magic and miracles when they happen. Then, when I write about them in my journal, I'm telling the Universe, in effect, that I appreciate the surprise and I'm open to receiving more!

When my husband is walking toward the door most mornings, I usually remind him to "look for the magic and miracles in today and call me when you get one!" It doesn't happen often, but I do love it when he calls and says, "You won't believe what just happened…" and then regales me with an incredible story.

Magic and miracles can be subtle, or even, you might say, a coincidence—like today, when I was driving back to my office at home and thinking that I needed to call someone to gather more information for a price quote I was putting together. I got home, flipped open my laptop to check emails, and voilà: there was the information from the person I was planning to call in an email, complete with an attached visual. I called her and said, "I love it when this stuff works. I just thought of calling you to ask about this, and voilà, here it is!" That happens more times than not to me. I can be thinking of someone intently and then I get a phone call from them. I always laugh and let them know that they "got" my call—we are all connected in ways that we can't see. The mental "call" or thought can be just as effective as dialing the number.

I often consider the beauty of the natural world that surrounds us as an example of the magic and miracles of everyday life. It's noticing the sky filled with colorful puffy clouds after a rainstorm washes through at sunset. (I took a picture of the sky and then did a watercolor of it to capture the beauty.) The sweet fragrance of jasmine flowers while out on a morning walk, the full moon rising as it illuminates the night sky—these are the things that I think of as magic and miracles.

One of my favorite magic and miracle stories is about our cats. Years ago our dog Wendy, the sweetest black lab, had to be put down when she was about 12 years old due to hip dysplasia, tumor growth, and other ailments. Our house seemed so empty without our girl to greet us at the door, often with a shoe in her mouth. We missed her lumbering up the stairs, following us wherever we'd go. The kitchen seemed empty at meal times with no Wendy begging at the table, her mouth open, tongue out and panting, waiting for any scraps to be tossed her way. I missed my walking/running companion, too, but I also knew that even though the kids, teenagers then, wanted another dog, I did not want to go through the training/puppy stage with a new dog.

A few months passed and it was now Christmastime. I had been considering getting a kitten. Kittens don't require the time and energy that a puppy does, but they can still offer the warmth and love of an animal companion. That December my office had a holiday party at a restaurant. I was seated next to the husband of one of my coworkers. Somehow I began telling him the story of having to put Wendy down and how difficult it was for my two kids and me. We missed her presence; yet, as I explained, I didn't want another dog but had just begun to think about getting a kitty for Christmas. He got excited and told me about a coworker of his who fostered kittens. This coworker and his wife were looking for a good home for two calico sisters they had been fostering since the fall.

The next day I called his office and was put in touch with the foster dad. We made plans for me to come and meet the kitties. They were very intent on making sure whoever adopted the sisters would keep them together and would give them a good home. I couldn't keep it a secret any longer, and it was within a week of Christmas, so I told Emily. She accompanied me on the kitty visit. It took no time at all for us to decide that these kittens were going to be ours. I honestly can't recall whether we brought them home that day or not, but I do know that when we finally got them home they filled the hole in our hearts that Wendy had left. Gigi and Gato kept us entertained for countless hours, as only kittens can. They were a miracle, bringing their unique kitty playfulness and love back into our home that Christmas. Seven years later, when I was leaving to move to San Francisco, Emily informed me that I would not be taking "the girls" with me. She was adamant that they stay with her in Seattle. And they did!

- Be on alert for magic and miracles in your every day life.

- Record the incidents so you'll remember them later.

> Miracles, in the sense of phenomena we cannot explain, surround us on every hand: life itself is the miracle of miracles.
> —GEORGE BERNARD SHAW,
> playwright

chapter twelve

Write a Letter and Mail It

When was the last time you sat down with a paper and pen and wrote a letter? Not only writing it but finding an envelope, addressing it, affixing a stamp, and dropping it the mail? I'll bet it's been so long you can't even remember the last time. What does this have to do with unlocking your creativity, you might ask? I believe that it's a creative act to write a letter—and sadly, one that is becoming a lost art. It is a rare day that you'll find a personal note or letter or card in your mailbox. Yet, if you do receive one, it could make your entire day. The fact that someone thought enough of you to actually drop a line in the mail means so much more than it used to mean. With email and tweets, communication can be instantaneous, but there's something different about holding a letter in your hand, relishing the penmanship of the letter writer. That letter can be read and reread. It can be placed in your journal for safekeeping. It might be written on special stationery or a card that has the perfect message for you. Thoughtfulness typically prevails when a letter is sent or received.

It was when I was scribbling ideas fast and furious for a calendar proposal I was working on that the idea floated into my head of writing a letter a week for the month of February. I thought: how appropriate to share with someone, especially someone who wouldn't be expecting it, a "real" letter telling them how much they were loved. Letters offer a chance for you to explore creative writing as you find the words that express your feelings in a poem or tell a story of a favorite memory of a moment shared with your beloved. Sending them in February, the month of love, would be very appropriate. Even more fun might be to send a note of love for no reason, other than that you want to let someone know you care enough to make time in your day to drop a line, say in the month of August or April! What a surprise to receive and a joy to send.

Do you know someone who is struggling with health issues? A card with the message "Thinking of you" can mean so much. When I was in college, my dad would often write me a quick note of encouragement and drop it in the mail. I found some of his notes a while back. Seeing his handwriting allowed me to "hear" his voice as if he were talking to me. I smiled as I reread the notes and thanked him right then for his thoughtfulness, knowing he could probably hear me, wherever he was, having been gone from this world for over 10 years. Letters live on.

Do you have a stack of notecards tucked away in a drawer? When I sell my cards at various events, I often have people purchase three or more, and they tell me that they love to have cards on hand that they can send one out at any time. What a great idea. They are prepared to acknowledge an occasion, send out a thank-you, congratulate an achievement, or just send love at the drop of a hat. Card and envelope are at the ready, just a few short words in their own handwriting, a stamp added, and they will make someone's day—not to mention, feel the good feelings that come from doing a good deed.

- Mail a letter and make someone's day!
- Take the month of February and send a letter a week to a different person you love. Tell them why.
- If you enjoy your letter writing in February, try it at various other times of the year.

A letter is always better than a phone call. People write things in letters they would never say in person. They permit themselves to write down feelings and observations using emotional syntax far more intimate and powerful than speech will allow.

—ALICE STEINBACH,
Educating Alice: Adventures of a Curious Woman

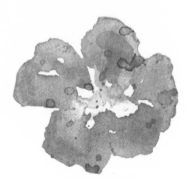

chapter thirteen

Get Lost in a Good Book

I'm still lost in the story of the book I just completed, *Flight Behavior*, by Barbara Kingsolver. It's a novel that left me questioning climate change, the precarious relationships of family and destiny, and how concepts you read about in a book may follow you throughout your life whether you are aware of it or not. There is absolutely nothing better (well, maybe a nap) than reading for hours on end, curled up in your favorite chair, sofa, bed, or hammock on a day begging for relaxation. One can enter a completely different world through a book.

Like a great movie, the story line stays with me, asking me to consider what might have happened to the characters as time marched on, the novel having ended. I question decisions the characters made, and simultaneously see how my own decisions brought me to places I would never have planned on my own. Is that how destiny works? Is it a calling? How is it our individual journeys unfold in ways we could never have imagined? As it is in a good book, the story line takes over in our individual lives, if we allow it, and we are guided by grace to live our brilliance. In *Flight Behavior* there is often fear of an unknown future looming, but a call persists and the characters can no longer deny their unique gifts and talents. The clarion call that urges them to return to school, or grab their art supplies, or learn to cook nutritious meals—any number of twists and turns happen when you let yourself change and grow. And it is all so fun to do when inspired by a book!

From my perspective, sitting on my couch, I can look over at two tall bookcases, purchased from Ikea years ago, that are overflowing with books. The Ikea bookshelves I liked because they were 18 inches deep rather than the standard 12 inches. More depth for stacking, I quickly discovered. You can line up books vertically along the back of the shelves, and then have room for another pile of horizontal books, which quickly grows in front of the vertical ones. I look at a stack of books, three of them authored by the same person. When I was reading those books, I was contemplating her message of love. I marveled at how she wove a story line of historical fiction together with a modern-day mystery that kept my head in the books till I'd finished all three. Each was a thriller, yet they also jarred my thinking about how the history of life can be altered when written. The lesson I learned is that love indeed conquers all, if we can only allow ourselves to be open to it. Those books reminded me of the miracles that can happen when living from your heart.

Then there are two books given to me by my mother-in-law, who also likes to read. These books were memoirs written by someone who was also raised in small-town Indiana. Funny and poignant, Haven Kimmel's books, *A Girl Named Zippy* and *She Got Up Off the Couch*, trace her own childhood—encompassing everything from the minutia of everyday living in a family to the desires that rose in her mom and inspired her to return to school, achieving a dream that was cut short by a pregnancy in her teen years. Not only did her mother finish college; she paved the way for her inquisitive daughter to chart her own heart path.

Books have always captivated me, transporting me to new worlds, introducing me to new concepts, teaching me to consider varying opinions about life, and truly opening up my limited world. My brother used to tease me when I was little about being a bookworm. Back then the term had a negative connotation, but it was appropriate for a bespectacled young girl who read constantly (unlike my brother). I still read constantly. Books are stacked on both sides of the bed: fiction, nonfiction, it doesn't really matter. My world is much larger because of all I've learned through books. And today, I welcome the term *bookworm*!

- When was the last time you read a good book? What did it teach you? Were you inspired to continue learning? Did you research anything on Google while you read?

- Get lost in a good book and find new ideas, worlds, and life waiting to be explored!

> For one who reads, there is no limit to the number of lives that may be lived, for fiction, biography, and history offer an inexhaustible number of lives in many parts of the world, in all periods of time.
>
> —LOUIS L'AMOUR,
> American author of Western novels

chapter fourteen

Keep a Journal

I'm sure you've heard the suggestion a million times before: "Write it out of you." I've been encouraging people to keep a journal for as long as I can remember. The reason I do so is that I know, firsthand, the power of writing things out of you, or as Julia Cameron put it so appropriately in her book *The Right to Write*, you can "right" things by writing about them. There is a power in just taking pen to paper and allowing the words to flow out of your mind and onto the page. It is a release, an outlet, a way for your emotions to find expression. Confusion in my mind can become unraveled when I begin to write. It's as if a big ball of tangled-up string begins to unroll itself and you can grab onto the end of the string, pulling it to find clarity. Wisdom pours forth, and more often than not, I can find my own answers as I pour out my problems onto the page. What may appear as a large, lurking problem is reduced to a reasonable situation that can be dealt with any number of ways once it is committed to paper.

Journals can record a lot more than your thoughts or events of the day. My journals hold a slice in time. Part sketchbook, part scrapbook (which is why I prefer blank pages to lined), my journals tell stories of places I visit, people I meet, situations I'm struggling with, an event that I want to remember forever, little daily tidbits, and the joys of magic and miracles experienced on any given day. They hold ticket stubs, postcards, pieces of paper with quotes that I liked—and sometimes I slip photos in for safe-keeping. I do quick sketches when out and about. It's a great way to capture memories via a sketch rather than words. My little travel watercolor case often accompanies me in my backpack, so I can add color. Sometimes I'm working out an idea for a painting, which I will complete later.

At one time, it seemed I had journals all over the place. I had a designated dream journal to capture my dreams of the night, a gratitude journal to write down the five things I was grateful for each day, and a workout journal where I jotted down distance and time of workouts—not to mention my ongoing journal! Too many journals, but I wasn't as disciplined as I needed to be to keep them all running. So instead, I've gone back to pretty much using one journal for everything. I still have a separate one for the gratitude recordings.

I've got boxes of journals in the basement. Writing this chapter inspired me to go downstairs and grab a few journals. Time flies by as I open and read various entries, reliving moments long past. I read about people from 12 years ago and struggle to remember who there were. I find a picture of my son from his first communion, a ticket stub from the Museum of Glass in Tacoma, which I visited while on a date, and a handout from one of my shaman classes. I marvel at how totally different my life is today than it was all those years ago. In one entry, I wrote, "Just watched '7 Years in Tibet' with Em. It's a very compelling story. Really makes me see that small decisions or actions we take can have a great effect many years later." So true, I think. In looking back from the perspective of today, I can see so many decisions I've made, however small, that continue to play out today.

I've found that I write in my journal at different times: when I'm happy, sad, joyful, upset, worried, needing help, or want to ask for guidance. (See chapter 3, Write with Your Nondominant

Hand.) I sketch daily life, the cats, fruit in a bowl, trees and land-scapes I see when I walk, and always the plane waiting at the gate when I'm about to fly anywhere. I opened a journal from 1989 and found a little sketch titled "Spring Flowers and Grass," with the date 4.8.89 next to it. I was quickly transported back to the park where I made the sketch. Journals can hold so much of who we are, not only a receptacle of our life but a powerful tool for assistance in transformation as well.

When I suggest the tool of journal writing to find clarity with life, people ask me, "How often do you write?" I always answer that there's no one way to write, at least for me. Sometimes it's daily, maybe even a few times a day, then not for a week. Or maybe every four days. Trust yourself to know when and how often to break open that notebook.

- Try keeping a journal for a period of time. Does it become a habit?

- Become an observer of life. Like a reporter, you can carry your notebook with you and make notations of details you don't want to forget, and then flesh out the story later.

Whether you're keeping a journal or writing as a medi-tation, it's the same thing. What's important is you're having a relationship with your mind.

—NATALIE GOLDBERG,
Writing Down the Bones

chapter fifteen

Clean Out Your Closets

I t's been said many times that if you want to bring in the *new*, you've got to make room for it. Which translates to: get rid of the *old*! Go through your closets, go through your drawers, go through the nooks and crannies and clean up, clear out, and make way for life to surprise you! "Pitch, purge, and pack" became a mantra of mine as I went through 19 years of memories (i.e., stuff!) in my big old house in Seattle. I had gotten married a year earlier, and for a variety of reasons, my new husband wanted to return to San Francisco, where he had lived for many years prior to our marriage. (He had transferred with his job to Seattle.) Thankfully, he wanted me to accompany him to San Francisco. It was a big decision, one we didn't take lightly.

But in retrospect, we realized that we really had no idea of what that decision meant for us. We really had no clue about the extent of work that would be required to fix up my house to make it ready for the real estate market. We started in by simply delegating areas each week to focus on. We had a number of projects going on for an entire summer and much of the fall. We power-washed the patio, cut back trees and shrubs, took multiple trips to the dump and to Goodwill, hired help to replace the floorboards of the front porch, had a new sidewalk poured. We sanded, painted, washed, and scrubbed. The work seemed endless. I found myself having difficulty letting go of many of the memories. "I can't throw away the moo-cow sheets, we got those when Bob was a little guy." (By then he was then 23.) Mark, being objective, would ask me a few questions and then provide very logical reasoning for why it did not make sense to keep whatever it was I wanted to hold onto. It was a challenge, but it was also liberating. When it was all over and done, we had downsized from a large four-bedroom home to a two-bedroom apartment. It was a valuable exercise to determine what was essential and what could go.

As I cleaned up and cleared out 19 years of living, my entire life shifted. I began to view myself differently. I had referred to myself as a corporate sales queen and single mom for so long that I didn't realize that I would be releasing those labels when I also released the hold on my old life. It took some time before I got a handle on a new label that would resonate with me, an artist/entrepreneur living in San Francisco. As a whole new life unfolded, I was able to birth the creative life that had been longing to burst forth. I'm convinced that had I not gone through the difficult process of transformation, I wouldn't have had the chance to spread my wings and flutter into the creative life that was waiting for me.

You don't have to completely make over your entire life to see change. It can be as easy as cleaning out your closets. Don't overwhelm yourself with the thought that this Saturday is the day to finally tackle the closets. Take a few Saturdays in a row. Maybe only an hour or two each time, and maybe another month or two will pass before you go at it again. Trust yourself to know when to get in and dig around. Make it an adventure—clean out a dresser drawer a night for a week straight. Be diligent about pitching what no longer fits you physically or what no longer works (like that old remote). We have a tendency to hold onto things, but honestly, holding onto the past can clog up the plumbing. Just like the Roto Rooter plumber who makes the water run through the pipes with ease when he clears out the drain—as you clean out your closets, dressers, basements, and such, things will flow easier into and out of your life. As they say, "One man's junk is another man's treasure." Drop off a bag or two at Goodwill and see what good comes into your life in another form! Watch and record what new things come into your life after cleaning up the old.

- Designate a spot where you can place a few laundry baskets. They can be labeled "pitch," "purge," and "pack." Be diligent about dropping clothes and other items into the baskets. When they get filled, dispose of appropriately.

- Record what happens as you move through this process. It may help you to document what you let go of—you can jot down five places you wore that favorite dress before you drop it into the Goodwill bag or draw a sketch of that lamp you got for a wedding present (the first time). You'll keep the good memories, but letting go of the object allows room for the *new* to move in!

You can find a lot of old memories when you clean out your closet.

—(UNKNOWN)

chapter sixteen

Create Sacred Space

A sacred space is a designated place that you can go to for renewal, introspection, and reflection—a place to call your own, where you can reenergize your spirit, refresh your thinking, and enjoy the peace and quiet of your own personal sanctuary. You can meditate, write in your journal, stretch and do yoga, or use it for your creative endeavors. It can be an entire room, or the top of a dresser that becomes your altar, or any size space in between. I recall a friend telling me that she used her closet for her meditation space. It worked for her; it was quiet, and she could go in and sit by herself away from the noise and busyness of the household. That closet doubled as a sacred space.

Over the years I've created many sacred altars and sacred spaces. I have a dresser that for years has doubled as an altar, holding objects sacred to me: photos of my children, wishing rocks and seashells I picked up at various beaches, candles, statues of angels, notes of my dreams, affirmations, and prayers, and ongoing artwork. It provides a touchstone during the morning as I prepare for the day. As I stand in front of it for a few moments and allow my eyes to rest on a memento, an overflowing of good feelings washes over me.

Before I create a painting, I create a sacred space by lighting candles. As I strike the match and watch the flame burn bright,

I silently send up a prayer asking for help from above with my work. I believe in divine inspiration, and lighting my candles puts the Divine on alert that I'll be requesting her guidance and assistance as I depict my subject.

A very comfortable chair becomes my sacred space on mornings when I sit in it cross-legged to begin my meditation. I've watched magnificent sunrises from my perch in the chair and noted how the light changes: at 6:00 a.m. in the winter it is completely dark, but at 6:00 a.m. in the summer I'm bathed in the light of day. Witnessing the sunrise is part of my morning ritual—it contributes to the sense of the sacred in life as I sit comfortably ensconced in my chair.

- I realize that I have a number of sacred spaces: my blue chair, my dresser, the candles on the dining table. At various points my sacred spaces double as mundane places. I realize that it's the energy I bring to the space that determines how it will function.

- Where can you find a physical place (large or small, inside or out) that can become a sanctuary for you to retreat to?

- Once you determine an ideal spot, begin to personalize it. Make sure you have a comfortable place to sit. Then add your mementos, statues, and candles as well as live plants or flowers, if you like.

- Writing in your journal allows for the self-expression that a sacred space tends to cultivate. You can also consider listening to music or any sound that might encourage you to relax: a fountain, wind chimes, etc.

Your sacred space is where you can find yourself
again and again.

—JOSEPH CAMPBELL,
The Power of Myth

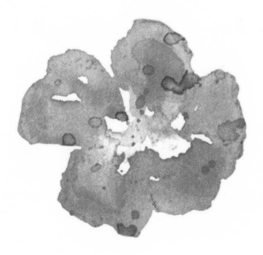

chapter seventeen

It's the Little Things

*Watch the fuchsia unfolding... Listen to the birds
chirping... Relish the moments... It's the Little
Things in Life... Take notice... Don't let daily
delights slip by.*

—FAVORITE SENTIMENTS
FROM A GREETING CARD I CREATED

We sometimes can get so focused on accomplishing our goals, or crossing off items on a long to-do list, or caught up in the drama of life, that we totally miss the little things. And yet, if we allow ourselves the gift of relishing the tiny moments, without any effort we'll be living in the present, more apt to appreciate all the little things in life that make life so worthwhile. Like the birds chirping as you stretch upon awakening on an early spring morning; the sunset as it dips below the horizon; the laughter of a baby; the hug you get when you greet your friend.

Recently I had the opportunity to walk one of my favorite labyrinths as I delivered an order for my cards at Mercy Center in Burlingame, California. It is a retreat center that has a lovely contemplative garden with a labyrinth, a statue of St. Francis, a

Celtic cross, and various benches to sit on. As I began to walk the well-worn circular paths, I noticed the birdsong. They seemed to be talking with all their different chirps, trills, and warbles. I wondered what they were saying. I walked past a jasmine plant and buried my nose in it, inhaling the sweet scent. Peace was descending into my body as I walked, taking in the sounds and smells of nature. I sat on a bench afterward to take a few moments to write in my journal.

I was inspired to do a quick sketch of the garden as well. As I was leaving, a cascading bunch of white flowers on a large bush captivated me. I stopped to take a photo with my phone, making it my screen wallpaper after capturing just the right view. What a lovely afternoon, filled with little delights that made my day.

As the lyrics to Rodgers and Hammerstein's song "My Favorite Things" remind us—as sung by Maria (played by Julie Andrews) in *The Sound of Music*—it's the little things that make us smile, wash away our troubles, and leave us feeling like there's nothing we can't do. I love that song. "Raindrops on roses and whiskers on kittens!" It's filled with joyful appreciations for life's little pleasures. We should all be so lucky as to dance and sing each day about the good that is everywhere, and relish the things that delight us.

- List the little things you've noticed over the past few days that make you smile.

- What happens when you become conscious of the little things?

- Commit to noticing little things each day, and write about them or share them with someone.

> It has long been an axiom of mine that the little things
> are infinitely the most important.
>
> —ARTHUR CONAN DOYLE,
> *The Adventures of Sherlock Holmes*

chapter eighteen

Dream REALLY Big!

For many years I had a piece of paper posted on my fridge that asked this question: "If you could do anything and money wasn't an object, what would you do?" I'd read that and answer to no one in particular, "I'd have a greeting card company," or "I'd work in my garden and paint pictures, living a creative life," never imagining that someday I'd be doing all three. At that time, I was a Corporate Sales Queen, as I used to refer to myself. Though I thought it would be great fun to invent this new persona, I had no idea how I would do it. You've got to dream big. Don't try to figure out how the dream will appear. Just hold the image in your mind and let the Universe, God, magic, whatever you call it, surprise you with an outcome that will certainly exceed your wildest dreams.

I was meditating the other day and got the image of the walls of a box falling away. I was in the box watching the walls fall backward. Then there stretched an expansive vista in all directions. I realized, at that moment, that the limitations I experience are the walls of the box. It's my box. My walls. In order for me to have this BIGGER life that I dream of, I have to let the walls of my self-imposed limitations fall away and breathe in the expansive view just waiting for me.

I ask myself, Can I really do it? I question and doubt and become so frustrated, and yet when I finally allow myself to be in that space of dreaming really big, I often see immediate results.

The seeds we plant grow and flourish. My dad was in sales, and I followed in his footsteps. I wasn't selling frozen pork bellies (my dad was a stockbroker and a commodities trader), but rather office furniture and then commercial carpet. Yet common to sales is the need to be motivated and to stay motivated, to believe in the product you are representing and to serve your customer. My dad read books by Dale Carnegie and Norman Vincent Peale and listened to the tapes of Earl Nightingale. He motivated himself in the days before an entire industry grew up and flourished around programs like "The Secret." He also planted the seeds of inspiration and motivation in me. I was lucky enough to have him give me many of his books and tapes. From *Think and Grow Rich*, by Napoleon Hill, to *The Magic of Thinking Big*, by David J. Schwartz, to a series of cassette tapes by the father of motivation himself, Earl Nightingale, I was gifted with tools that would allow me to flourish as well as develop an appreciation and lifelong love for motivational books and inspirational stories.

A message that runs through all of these books, programs, CDs, and magazines is the power of dreaming big: believing in yourself, knowing you can live a dream. Belief is the key to making the dream manifest. Believe you can have it. Knock down the walls of your limitations and watch out for surprises as coincidences begin to show up, along with magical moments of synchronicity!

- Write a paragraph or two or three describing your big dream. Engage all your senses as you create the dream. What aromas drift by? What is the temperature? How do you feel? Are you dancing for joy? Singing to the high heavens? What colors do you see? Can you taste the sweetness of your experience? Describe it in detail. Have fun and play around with descriptive words.

- If you could do anything and money wasn't an object, what would you do?

- Post that question on your refrigerator and let the answers marinate in your psyche, knowing and trusting that someday they'll manifest as that really BIG dream!

Rise above little things. Be a big thinker. You are what you think. So just think big, believe big, act big, dream big, work big, give big, forgive big, laugh big, image big, love big, live big, carry that list and you'll start feeling big. Be a believer and you'll be an achiever.

—MIKE GEORGE,
creator of "Thought for the Day" emails

chapter nineteen

Act "As If"

I don't recall the title of the book I was reading when I first encountered the idea of acting "as if," but I do remember it had a profound effect on me. The concept was such an intriguing one: if you could simply act as if you had already achieved what you wanted, or act as if you were the kind, benevolent person you wanted to be, then kindness and benevolence would be extended to everyone you met. You could even employ the "act as if" philosophy to assist you in creating incredible relationships. Because, as I realized, if you treated the relationship as you'd like it to be, acting as if, then you'd experience it in just that manner. It all made sense to me, but it was a bit challenging to implement.

"Begin with the End in Mind" is Habit #2 in Stephen Covey's popular book, *The 7 Habits of Highly Effective People.* How does it work, beginning with the end in mind? Covey's Habit #2 basically states that you see the end result first, in your mind's eye. There is a principle that all things are created twice: first mentally, and second by being created in the physical world. Just as a blueprint provides the plans and direction for a building to rise out of the ground, so do our thoughts hold the plans that will become the events and people in our day-to-day life.

Stephen Covey encourages the development of a Personal Mission Statement. Creating one will focus you to consider, and then plan for, what you want to be and do. It becomes your personal blueprint for success. Your Mission Statement will allow you to "see" your own destiny clearly and secure the future you envision. You've got to see it to believe it, as the saying goes. But first you have to imagine it in your mind's eye, or "act as if" it's already here.

Another author I've admired for years who also preaches the power of acting "as if" is Mike Dooley. I listened to Mike's CD set, *Infinite Possibilities: The Art of Living Your Dreams,* a few years ago. I loved how he kept reminding us to focus on the end result and stop worrying about "the cursed hows"—those questions we torment ourselves with, such as, "How is this going to happen?" "How can I figure this out?" and "How will it look?" We are not meant to figure it out; we are meant to have faith. And once our faith is rooted in acting "as if," that is when the seemingly impossible suddenly becomes possible.

A case in point: about two years ago, I was growing my little line of greeting cards called "Words and Watercolors." I was doing everything with the exception of printing the cards, and knew that I could not keep up with filling all the orders, then taking them to UPS or the post office. I needed help with fulfillment. And though I really enjoyed working with Ken of H&H Imaging, the printer who printed my cards digitally, I knew I needed to find a printer who could print offset. That would allow me to reduce my cost per card, which I needed to do to become more profitable. Boxes of cards were lining the hallway, and our second bedroom was the inventory storage.

Three large shelving units held cardboard boxes, which held the 5 x 7 greeting cards, stacked in the various categories of birthday, comfort, thank-you, etc. I was beginning to wonder where the new cards would go once I added more designs to the line. Inventory was definitely an issue—I was running out of room. I began considering how I could solve this issue as well.

Let me mention that although I agree with not trying to solve the cursed hows, I do believe it is important to engage in exploring options for solutions. I began talking to different people about fulfillment solutions. I was referred to a few other offset printers and began the task of interviewing them to find out if any would be the ticket for me. And last, I began praying for a "benevolent benefactor" because I knew I needed some financial help with this endeavor that seemed to be growing.

Every day, I'd visualize the end in mind and act as if it was all going to work out. (Believe me, I did have my share of doubt and worry, as I continue to do today, even though I know better.) I continued to reaffirm the three things I "knew" were coming: fulfillment help, an offset printer, a benevolent benefactor. I thought they would be three separate answers to my problems. This is where it can be fun to "act as if": when the answers do arrive, they are always more interesting and amazing and even elegant than anything you may contrive. And that's just what happened to me. One day I was talking to Ken and mentioned that I was ready to move from digital printing to offset. He asked if I had talked to John Frisch with Leewood Press. I said no. He suggested I do so and said I could use his name as a referral. A few days later, when I went to meet John at Leewood Press, I was happy to discover the address was on Indiana Street. I thought that was a good sign since I grew up in Indiana! The amazing thing was that John not only became my offset printer, his company does fulfillment for me and all of Words and Water-colors inventory is easily housed in an office that once sat empty. It's now lined with deep shelves on three walls. I could never have come up with a solution as elegant as that. All the answers were rolled into one!

Pretending is the fastest way to believing, and believing is the fastest way to receiving.

—MIKE DOOLEY,
Infinite Possibilities

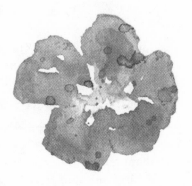

chapter twenty

Act on Inspiration

When that subtle idea floats through your consciousness, act on it! I know from experience that as quickly as the idea comes, it can be elusive and can dissipate if not caught and made concrete into words or drawings. What ideas do you want to capture? What dream begs to be written down before it dissolves back to the ether? (I got this idea while out walking and captured it in the notes on my iPhone.)

You can add these flashes of inspiration to your journal. By doing so you'll be able to build on ideas, possibly creating a future short story or poem, a song or a recipe, a pattern for a quilt, or socks you want to knit. Any number of projects can be started—all because you caught the inspiration as it drifted by and recorded it in some fashion.

There's really no way you can prepare to act on inspiration; you just have to commit yourself to noticing when a thought, idea, or flash of inspiration floats by and you'll immediately capture it as it does. Besides making notes on my iPhone, I've used the voice recording feature to capture ideas while driving. Just hold up the phone and talk into it, recording the idea. It's that easy. I can even hear the excitement for the idea in my voice as I replay the message. I know some writers who never leave home without a little pocket notebook. Astute at observing the daily life that surrounds them, they have their handy pocket notebook available so they can jot down a few lines that later can be transcribed to a short story.

Famous inventors Thomas Edison, Nikola Tesla, and Albert Einstein all knew the power of inspiration. It is said that Nikola Tesla had flashes of insight so intense that plans for his inventions appeared whole in his head at once, in every detail. A flash of inspiration can be like that. It comes to you whole. Inspiration, the word itself, offers a clue to where the bursts of insight originate, in spirit. The two words, *inspiration* and *spirit*, share a common origin in the Latin word meaning "to breathe." Call it what you will, the Divine, angels and guides, the void, God/Goddess; however you refer to it, know that spirit has gifted you with an idea that can be made, explored, played with, or built. It may take some work, as Edison famously noted:

> *Genius is one percent inspiration and 99 percent perspiration.*

But the work is always worth the effort!

- Declare that you will capture an idea and act on it.
- Once you do it, try it again!
- Remember a time when you acted on an inspired idea. Write about what you did, how it felt, what you created as a result. Did you share your creation with others?

chapter twenty-one

Go to a Play

M y husband and I are fond of plays. We've discovered that going to a play is a totally different experience than going to watch a movie. Both are entertaining and both typically tell stories, but when you go to a play you have to engage your imagination. A movie explicitly shows every detail, often more graphically than needed, to explore the plot and engage the viewer. In a play, the stage is set to provide a backdrop for the action/drama, but your imagination fills in the missing details. For instance, you might hear a whistle blow, but you won't see a train rolling down the tracks. You imagine the couple seated, their baggage overhead, as they shyly glance at each other. Strangers at the beginning of the long train trip, you discover from the story line of the play, they will become infatuated with each other by the end of the trip. They meet on the train and subsequently court and get married. The play is told in a series of flashbacks, so the whistle blowing, at various times, always brings you back to the beginning of their life together, the magic of their first encounter. You "see" it all in your mind's eye, while the stage of the theater is set in their current living room, to reflect their unglamorous life 40 years later. So went the story line of a play that we saw a number of years ago. It stayed with us, as plays often do.

When we were first married, we often found ourselves going

to plays. Living in Seattle then, we frequented a small regional theater in West Seattle as well as ACT, a contemporary theater acclaimed for introducing new works, and the 5th Avenue Theatre, which performed Broadway shows. We attended everything. It was uncanny, we noted, that when we went to see a play, we often found ourselves watching our own struggles and circumstances. It became humorous at times, uncomfortable at others, to see played out on stage the challenges we were facing in our own marriage. It was as if the mirror provided by the actors was reflecting back to us our own issues. The universal themes—anger, fear, love, commitment, trust—were explored on stage as well as in our lives. I have to say that going to see those plays helped us tremendously. It provided a platform for our own discussions.

Just the other night, we stepped out to see *Can You Dig It?* at The Marsh, a breeding ground for new theatrical performance. Don Reed wrote and performed a one-man show that recounted his youth, growing up in Oakland in the 60s when his family was whole. As his website attests, "Before his father became a pimp—before his mother reluctantly became a Jehovah's Witness—a lot of wonderful, scary, amazing, unnecessary, cool, moving, unbelievably *true* stories unfolded." Reed's portrayal of all the characters that populated his formative years was very funny and poignant. The music of the 60s appropriately set the tone. I laughed so hard I nearly cried at times—and at the end I did cry when those characters, which had come to life with his outstanding storytelling abilities, were put to rest.

- When was the last time you saw a play? Find one that looks inviting and buy tickets.

- Enjoy the performance and hold a postperformance discussion with your fellow attendees. Was the play relevant for you in any way? What did you learn? How did the play inspire you? Challenge you? Move you?

- Write your own play!

> We can see the film stars of yesterday in yesterday's films, hear the voices of poets and singers on a record, keep the plays of dead dramatists upon our bookshelves, but the actor who holds his audience captive for one brief moment upon a lighted stage vanishes forever when the curtain falls.
>
> —DAPHNE DU MAURIER,
> *The "Rebecca" Notebook and Other Memories*

chapter twenty-two

Laugh

t's said that laughter is the best medicine. And it is true. Entire books have been written on the virtues of the healing power of laughter. In 1979, Norman Cousins wrote the ground-breaking book *Anatomy of an Illness,* which charted his own startling recovery from a severe illness to health. Not only did he self-prescribe hours of humorous television shows to watch, he took an active role in his own health with the positive relation-ship he developed with his physician. Truly he was a model for many others in developing a therapy based on humor.

All sorts of healthy physical changes take place in your body as you erupt into laughter. A good sense of humor can literally save your life, as Cousins notes in his book. Laughter has been shown to:

- Relax the whole body
- Boost the immune system
- Trigger the release of endorphins
- Protect the heart
- Add joy and zest to life
- Ease anxiety and fear
- Strengthen relationships
- Help defuse conflict

There are lots of reasons to see the comedy in situations we encounter as we go about our lives. When we can laugh at ourselves, we lighten our mood. We can gain insight as we approach a problem from a different perspective.

Earlier this year I found myself often sharing a very funny story about how I got a swollen upper lip, chipped front teeth, and a downright scary-looking face. My lighthearted approach to it not only made me feel better; I believe it contributed to my healing: barely a scar is noticeable now on my upper lip.

It all started when Mark and I read a book, *The Big Leap*, by Gay Hendricks, while on vacation in Florida. We were energized with the promise the book holds for "providing a clear path for achieving our true potential and attaining not only financial success but also success in love and life," as the back cover states. We embraced the affirmation "I expand in abundance, success, and love every day, as I inspire those around me to do the same," and repeated it often. However, in order to get to this point of expansion, one needs to identify and work with their Upper Limit problems.

As Gay Hendricks explains: "Each of us has an inner thermostat setting that determines how much love, success, and creativity we allow ourselves to enjoy. When we exceed our inner thermostat setting, we will often do something to sabotage ourselves, causing us to drop back into the old, familiar zone where we feel secure." A few typical Upper Limit behaviors: worrying, blame and criticism, getting sick or hurt, squabbling, hiding significant feelings, not keeping agreements, not speaking significant truths to the relevant people.

As the old year wound down and the New Year came into focus, I kept thinking about breaking through my Upper Limit. Wanting desperately to take The Big Leap and move forward into my zone of genius, I had my own mantra going in my head about making a breakthrough so I could have the incredible growth I wanted in the new year for Words and Watercolors, my greeting card business.

It was a day in mid-January, late in the afternoon, when I finally made it outside for a brisk walk. It was a beautiful, crisp, clear, sunny, blue-sky kind of day. I felt so energized that I thought I'd try jogging. I'd had problems with my left knee since the previous spring and had not jogged since. I was exhilarated as I jogged for the first time in nearly a year, so excited to be outside with the glow of a setting sun coloring the world a golden hue. I had made it about a mile from home, out to the India Basin Industrial Park, when suddenly I tripped. Splat. A face plant, as Mark called it. I was shocked when I sat up and found blood gushing onto my hands and the white fleece I was wearing. I could feel that my two front teeth were chipped—not just my two front teeth, but my new porcelain crowns that had recently been replaced on my two front teeth. Chipped. Thankfully an angel named Erica saw me fall and stopped her car, asking if I needed help and offering a ride. I told her I'd get blood in her car, and she handed me a box of Kleenex. I grabbed a bunch, held the wad up to my lip, and got in the car.

Thankfully also, Mark was home when I returned. In my distress, I asked him to call Dr. Petrini, our dentist. I had no inclination to go to the hospital until Dr. Petrini suggested it, after I explained what had happened and the fact that I was still bleeding even while holding an ice pack to my face. Off to St. Francis Emergency Room we went. When I walked out two hours later, I had 11 stitches in my upper lip and three on the inside of my upper lip. I asked Mark if he thought this was an Upper Limit problem. "No Peg, you fell."

But in the middle of the night, when I couldn't return to sleep, I kept replaying the events of the fall in my head. Finally I realized, "Oh my god, I had a breakthrough! I broke through my upper LIP!" I began laughing at the absurdity of it all. My upper lip was completely broken through. The doctor showed me how I could have done it with my teeth as I hit the pavement. Beware the power of words! I'd been asking to break through my upper limit. Well, I broke through my upper lip! I decided that I would touch my upper lip whenever I found myself opening the door of doubt, or worrying about things I couldn't change, or experiencing any other Upper Limit issues.

And for the rest of the story, as Paul Harvey used to say, I did go see Dr. Petrini the following week. He filed down the rough parts of my teeth and told me that I would have to replace the crowns. He suggested I return to the site of the fall and see how bad the sidewalk really looked. When I returned to the intersection, I gasped. There was a pipelike rod sticking up through the broken sidewalk. That's it! That was what I tripped on.

Being able to laugh about the entire situation and see it as an integral part of my strong desire to grow my business helped me accept the rather Frankenstein's monster-looking face I was sporting. Laughter is certainly powerful medicine. When I tell the story today, the stitches are barely visible!

- How often do you laugh, out loud, each day?
- Do you employ your sense of humor when looking at a situation?
- Go to a comedy club.
- Watch a funny movie or TV show.
- Do something silly and laugh hard!

I love people who make me laugh. I honestly think it's the thing I like most, to laugh. It cures a multitude of ills. It's probably the most important thing in a person.

—AUDREY HEPBURN

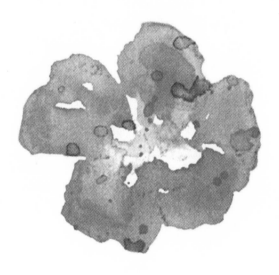

chapter twenty-three

Give Thanks

An attitude of gratitude is an essential component to living a life well imagined. By giving thanks and focusing on all the good in your life, you invite more of the same into your world. It's really a no-brainer, as they say.

What I found most surprising, when doing research for this chapter, were the findings from a study titled "The Research Project on Gratitude and Thankfulness." The co-investigators were Robert A. Emmons, University of California–Davis, and Michael E. McCullough, University of Miami. They write, "Gratitude is the forgotten factor in happiness research." Isn't that great? Your happiness increases in direct correlation to your attitude of gratitude! The study found that those who kept a gratitude journal enjoyed these benefits:

- Exercised more regularly, were healthier, slept better, and felt more optimistic
- Made more progress toward personal goals
- Were more alert and enthusiastic, and could handle stress more effectively
- Had a greater sense of feeling connected to others

Given those findings, who would not want to implement this simple and rewarding practice in their daily life? Just like Oprah, who has often advocated keeping a gratitude journal and each day listing five things to be grateful for, I, too, have witnessed the power and benefits that result. I've found that when I'm consistent with my gratitude practice, I'm more aware of the little things that surprise and delight me throughout the day. When life gets busy and I begin to feel out of control, it takes me a while to realize that I've not been taking the time to jot down my five points of gratitude daily. Right then I commit to getting back to noticing the things that bring joy and happiness into my world, and begin anew.

Recently I went through a rather rough patch with my emotions. I found I was comparing myself to others. I knew that was not the way to live an inspired life, but I couldn't help myself. No matter how ridiculous my crazy thoughts, I was having a tough time kicking myself back into first gear, so to speak, and moving forward. Instead I was stuck in neutral in a pity party world of whaaaaaaa, like a toddler whining about not having the toy he wants; I was not a happy camper. What finally helped me shift my perspective was the realization that I do, indeed, have a lot to be grateful for each and every day. I took the time to notice life's simple pleasures and the beauty that is everywhere. It worked. I witnessed a sky awash in colors and clouds painted by the sunrise each morning when I opened my eyes after meditating. The large lavender plant on my back steps perfumed the air with its spiky flowers, attracting the bees. The fragrance of a cup of jasmine tea in the morning, riding bikes with my husband along the waterfront: things to make me smile. Life is good, as the T-shirt company proclaims. Once again, I'm a grateful participant in life and giving thanks for all the good that comes with it!

We often think of giving thanks at Thanksgiving, but what

about the other 364 days of the year? I would like giving thanks to be a year-round practice. Granted, the entire month of November is typically designated the season of harvest and thanks, with magazine articles, radio, and TV full of heartwarming stories of gratitude, and lists and activities one can complete to celebrate the day of Thanksgiving. I created my own activity that my kids and I completed each Thanksgiving morning. We'd grab crayons, colored markers, and large sheets of newsprint. Then we'd gather in the front room and begin our drawings of what we were thankful for that year. It was always fun to see the finished pages of artwork filled with soccer balls, basketballs, our dog Wendy and cat George, plus other images of our lives back then. When I moved out of my home of 19 years, I found, behind a big bookcase, a stash of our newsprint sheets from various Thanksgivings. I wish I had saved at least one of them, but I was in my "pitch, purge, and pack" mode and they all were pitched.

Do you currently practice giving thanks for life's joys, surprises, delights—and yes, even the challenges? If you have a mindset that allows you to look for the good in all situations, you can often see the silver lining in the clouds that may be hovering. It's really a circle—having the attitude of gratitude allows one to be more optimistic. With an optimistic view of the world, you can see things in a more positive light, and from that viewpoint you are able to circle back around to being grateful for life's lessons you may be learning. Amazing how it all works!

- Purchase a journal that will be specifically for your gratitude exercises.
- Develop a practice of recording five things to be grateful for each day.
- See the good in all things and give thanks for even the smallest of wonders, like the breeze blowing

through an open window on a warm summer day.

- Just for fun, instead of writing your Thanksgiving list, draw it.

Without gratitude, happiness is rare. With gratitude, the odds for happiness go up dramatically.

—ZIG ZIGLAR,
motivational speaker

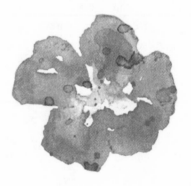

chapter twenty-four

Play with a Child

1 noticed, the other evening, the wide-eyed wonder toward all things in this world that a child exhibits. I was playing with T, short for Taylor, my neighbor who's fast becoming my favorite playmate. It's her spontaneous nature that I most love in T—it reminds me to loosen up, let go, and play with life!

I accompanied T to the little park a block away. She's only two, a petite little thing, but that didn't stop her from climbing onto the large play equipment. Running with delight, she touched and explored everything. Ooh, there's the wheel, turn turn turn, then up to the slide, turn around and down the slide on her tummy. "Wheeeeee." Off the slide and back around to the steps to climb up and do it all over again. She discovered that she can hold onto the railings and swing a bit—that's great fun—then head back down the stairs, saying "Look it, T down" as she walks down.

T was carrying her BoBo, her bear. BoBo was wearing a pair of pull-ups, and T discovered that when BoBo was thrown down on the ground, the wood chips stuck to the pull-ups. We brushed him off. T thought that was so much fun that she repeated the process again and again and again. It takes repetition to master a process, I thought to myself, and T is having a grand time throwing BoBo down, saying "BoBo got dirty," and brushing him off—only to repeat the process and laugh some more.

From the play equipment to the dogs that were frequenting

the park, we were busy going back and forth. One large dog, a black lab, was resting. He was kind enough to let T pet him. T got down on her haunches to stare intently into his eyes, a big grin forming as she'd point and smile, before taking off to head back to the playground equipment. There she once again climbed up the stairs, turned the wheel, went down the slide, and repeated around and around her unique repertoire of play.

I quickly remembered that being in the presence of a two-year-old activates the two-year-old inside you! Our inner child is still a big part of us—and loves to come out and play. So I took a turn at the wheel and a whoosh down the slide for good measure myself, to T's delight.

With childlike wonder, we might be open to seeing aspects of our own life differently. We might open ourselves up to ideas that have occurred to us but we haven't begun to work on yet. There is a curiosity that is prevalent in a two-year-old. Explore the world around you. Engage with it as if you were seeing it for the first time. How might you consider doing something differently? Feel the lighthearted, carefree world of a two-year-old. They can truly live "in the moment," not concerned with the things they can't control.

- Invite one of the children in your life (neighbor, niece or nephew, grandchild or friend) to the local park for inspired moments of play.

- Incorporate a spirit of play as you go through the activities of your day.

- Buy sidewalk chalk and invite the neighbor kids over to color on the sidewalk.

- Draw a hopscotch figure and take turns jumping through the squares.

We don't stop playing because we grow old; we grow old because we stop playing.

—GEORGE BERNARD SHAW,
playwright

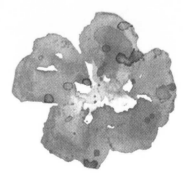

Discipline Yourself

I t is so true that dogged determination coupled with discipline is the key to achieving dreams. Discipline takes your desire out of the realm of hoping and dreaming and into the world of reality. Though we often associate discipline with drudgery and hard work, it can actually be something you look forward to each day. Try it. What would you like to improve in your life? What habit do you want to incorporate? What skill would you like to develop? Make a commitment to discipline yourself. Devote time to doing it, even if it is only 15 minutes a day. Carve out the time, and after a week you'll be surprised when you look back and see your accomplishments.

I've honed the art of discipline by making up "challenges" over the years. A challenge one year to draw or paint every day of my birthday month resulted in a few paintings that became best-selling cards in my Words and Watercolors line.

This year I started off by doing a painting a week. I would post them on Facebook so I could share with others. After posting paintings for three weeks in January, I realized that I was on to something. Knowing the power of discipline and the fun of a challenge for me, I declared that I would post a painting a week for the remainder of the year. I knew there would be weeks when that would really be a challenge to complete, but I can attest to the fact that by making a commitment to yourself and sticking with it, you accomplish things you never considered possible. I've stretched myself to complete a painting, not to mention stretched myself to try different papers and techniques. I'm learning, as I discipline myself, more about my own area of expertise.

A number of years ago I learned about the art of discipline and how challenges can be beneficial for you. Though I'd always been a jogger, I had a hard time keeping weight off after the birth of my children. My doctor recommended I try walking briskly every day for a minimum of 30 minutes. I didn't know how that would produce better results than my running a few times a week, but I accepted the challenge. That is when the birthday-month challenges began for me. I decided to try walking each day for the month of September. My motivation was to lose weight. I don't think I lost any significant weight, but I did enjoy the daily walks around my neighborhood with my dog Wendy by my side. And I was so pea-pickin' proud of myself for accomplishing the goal of getting exercise for 30 days straight. Each year after that, when the month of September rolled around, I would create a "birthday-month challenge" for myself, usually walking each day for the month or drawing or painting each day. One year I tried not eating chocolate for a month, but that didn't last. I realized that the challenge had to be something I enjoyed, not something that felt like deprivation.

Another tip for making discipline work is not to think in terms of the big picture: this often leads to feeling overwhelmed, which then leads to doing nothing. Instead I've found that breaking the activity down into chunks of time works wonders for me. For instance, often when I set out to do a painting, I'll set a time limit of an hour. If I choose to go over the hour, that's OK, too, but if I work in chunks of time I don't fall into the trap of thinking "I can't possibly do this." I've used time limits from 15 minutes up to a few hours. You can do anything for 15 minutes!

In my yoga class the other day, the instructor kept referring to the willful discipline it took to hold the poses. I liked how those two words sounded married together: willful and discipline. It was easier to hold a pose for a longer time incorporating the joy of willful discipline!

You may be surprised to find that you have already incorporated the act of discipline in your everyday life. Going to work each day is an act of discipline, as is caring for family or friends on a regular basis. Create a challenge for yourself, incorporate the art of discipline, and then be surprised at what you can accomplish!

- Challenge yourself to exercise on a regular basis.
- Commit to doing whatever it is you like to do but never find the time to do, even if it is for only 15 minutes a day.
- Be disciplined about eating healthy, discover nutritious recipes, and enjoy creating food that nourishes your body.
- Write about your experiences.

> Discipline yourself and others won't need to.
>
> —JOHN WOODEN,
> UCLA basketball coach

chapter twenty-six

Create a Collage

One of my favorite things to do: grab a bunch of magazines, glue, scissors, and foam core board and create the life I imagine! It's the perfect exercise to do in January as you "visualize" the new year, or around your birthday as you consider the next year of your life, or anytime you are going through change and transition or want to create a "vision board" on a particular project or subject. Creating a collage is not only fun; it can provide direction: you'll find yourself ripping out pictures and words that are meaningful to you, that call to you. Don't even think about what you are ultimately trying to create, just flip through the pages and rip, flip and rip, flip again until you amass enough paper to begin making a collage.

Last winter I had gathered a large stack of magazines, a variety that reflected my varied interests in watercolor/art, business success, lifestyle, and home and garden. It didn't take long before I had more than enough words and pictures lying around the table. I took scissors and homed in on the image or words that I wanted, cutting out what was peripheral. I began by selecting an anchor image, glued it down in the center of the foam core board, and built outward from there. I found numbers to spell out the year, and placed them underneath the anchor. The vision board came to life as images of interiors of a bungalow home joined a photo of a bedroom with a quilt on the bed (to celebrate the introduction of my first collection of quilting fabric this year, with Clothworks), and a picture of a woman in a yoga pose. I added more images: an English garden, destinations to visit, a woman running, a picture of a white feather, plus other interesting things of note. And then I laid the words, in a variety of fonts and colors, over the top: "The Nurture of Nature, Bursting, Breakthrough, Never Give Up, Optimism 101, Magic, Gift of Abundance, Strike a Balance."

I've created boards over the years with different themes or interests. I like to remind my husband, when we are out riding bikes and I look at him with his helmet on and his eyes smiling, that that is the exact image I pasted on one of my vision boards when I was "visualizing" a relationship. I had ripped out a photo of some guy with a bike helmet on, the angle of the photo showed the side of his face, there was that smile and those crinkly, lovely laugh lines round his eyes, the strap of the helmet coming down to buckle under the chin. It took me a while to put two and two together. It happened one day when were getting back on our bikes at a park. I had just taken a picture of Mark with my phone, and when I looked at it to save as his contact photo, I saw the same angle and image of that guy on my vision board from a few years earlier. *Holy Christmas!* There he is! It was uncanny to see the resemblance between my husband and some random guy I had pasted onto a vision board years earlier.

I'm still waiting for the cute little stucco bungalow that I posted on a collage a few years ago to show up as my home!

- Gather the materials and go at it! Flip, rip, and tear out the makings of a great life!

- Have a Create Your Best Year party! Invite friends over, asking them to bring magazines to share, their own foam core board, and scissors. You can provide the glue sticks.

A dream collage is pictures of your goals. It is like your future photo album.

—BO BENNETT,
Year to Success

chapter twenty-seven

Go to the Zoo

I told Emily, my daughter, that I wanted to visit Woodland Park Zoo with her when I got to Seattle last month. Emily loves going to the zoo; even now, in her 20s, she still gets excited with the anticipation of seeing all the animals and wildlife. As do I. So off we went on a warm Saturday afternoon in August. We got the sense that we probably didn't pick the ideal time to visit when we drove around the very crowded parking lot looking for an open parking space. And once inside the gate, we really questioned our timing, but we took it all in stride: the large number of strollers, the toddlers running amok with parents and grandparents trying to corral them, the noise level of all that activity. Developing patience as we waited for prime viewing spots for the African Savanna, we were rewarded when we saw the hippo, rolling in the mud; the zebra, with all of its stripes; and the giraffe standing tall and elegant as it lunched on leaves of a nearby tree.

I'm constantly in awe as I watch these animals. There is such diversity in the human family, which we experienced that day at the zoo, but even more diversity in the mammals, birds, and wildlife we encountered. It's a very inspiring place for me.

Woodland Park Zoo, in Seattle, was the first zoo to create an immersion exhibit, which allows visitors to actually sense they are in the animals' habitat; buildings and barriers are hidden and sights and sounds from the natural environments are recreated. It has won more Best National Exhibit awards from the Association of Zoos & Aquariums than any other zoological institution except the Bronx Zoo.

From the African Savanna, we strolled over to Tropical Asia to see the elephants. I'm always so impressed with the sheer size of the elephants. And yet, with their slow, deliberate movements they appear gentle. Only one elephant was visible; the others must have been hiding in their habitat. The elephant barn at the zoo looks like it was transported from Thailand itself, with its unique architecture. We weren't expecting to see the warty pig, but he did make us laugh as we stared at him.

On to the Northern Trail, where one of our favorite exhibits is the indoor viewing area. There we saw the river otters swimming playfully through the water and a large bear standing tall beyond the river. We turned around to see an elk, basking in the sun as he lounged in the large field. The span of his antlers was impressive. I was clicking away with my camera, not sure what I'd do with the look of the antlers, but I wanted to capture them.

We didn't stop at every exhibit, instead going to see our favorites, even though it had been a long time since either one of us had visited the zoo. Just walking around with all the other families was entertaining by itself. I didn't stop to do any quick sketches, but was prepared to do so, with my backpack complete with sketchbook/journal and travel watercolors. Instead, I let my camera capture the images of the day.

As we were completing our tour of the zoo, we went to the new Humboldt penguin exhibit. Talk about darling, cute, funny, delightful creatures! We took lots of pictures of the waddling little guys. Some were standing on the shore of their rocky habitat, while others were swimming around and around playfully in the large pool of water, with a rocky island in the middle, where one guy stood looking as if he were playing King of the Mountain.

I hope to do a watercolor soon inspired by these tuxedoed little penquins!

I'm also fascinated with the flamingos: their salmon-pink feather colors, the amazing balance they seem to strike effortlessly as they stand on one leg and balance their entire body weight, how they look clustered together. They were our last stop, and I probably took even more pictures of them and their habitat than anywhere.

It was a fun afternoon at the zoo and we were both content as we got back in the car and headed home to Emily's apartment.

- Write about your trip to the zoo. What were your favorite animals, and why?

- Capture in a photograph or sit and sketch your favorite animal/exhibit.

- When you return home, do some research on the most exotic animals you saw at the zoo.

Someone told me it's all happening at the zoo.

—PAUL SIMON,
singer/songwriter

chapter twenty-eight

Shift Your Perspective

*When you change the way you look at things, the
things you look at change.*

—WAYNE DYER

That quote has been a driving force for me since the day I heard Wayne Dyer discuss how changing his perspective on his relationship with his father changed his life in a dramatic way. It was a remarkable story that had me in tears as I listened to the coincidences and magic that seemed to conspire to bring him to confront his own feelings for his father, whom he had never met, and how the forgiveness that he found for his father provided a personal shift in his perspective. My husband and I were driving to Sacramento as we listened to the CD recording of Dyer's PBS special, where he discussed the idea of the power inherent in forgiveness. We learned a lot about how that one profound and powerful act of forgiveness for his father shifted not only his perspective, but his entire life. That is how powerful forgiveness can be.

I've decided to take a rather lighthearted approach to changing the way I look at things. Imagine shifting your perspective by looking at a situation from a totally different physical perspective. How to do that, you ask? Is there a hill where you live that you can walk up for a more expansive view of the surrounding area? Can you drive to an overlook and see a vista stretching before you, where you can begin to see a bigger picture? When was the last time you climbed a tree? Do you recall the exhilaration as you plotted your ascent? What branch to step on, and then the next, and the next as you climb higher and higher?

I hadn't given any thought to climbing trees in, oh, maybe 45 years or so, when I saw this amazing tree with limbs shooting out in all directions, many of them low to the ground, one day while on an urban hike in John McLaren Park in San Francisco. I wasn't consciously aware, either, of the fact that I had listed "climb a tree" as a possible chapter title for my book a few weeks before. Yet, here was this amazing Monterey Cypress tree, which beckoned me to climb with its inviting branches.

I flashed back to the days of my youth, when I could often be found up in the branches of the large oaks that grew to the side of our house. My brother and I used to challenge each other to go out on a limb quite far and then gently push down on the branch with our feet, shaking the limb up and down. It was quite thrilling.

As I began to climb the cypress, I felt the delight of my 10-year-old inner child, gauging where to step. I placed my foot on a branch as I reached overhead for another branch to hoist me upward. Repeating the process—placing my foot, reaching overhead, hoisting upward—I climbed. I didn't get too high in the tree, maybe 10–15 feet up. What an interesting perspective to view the park from this vantage point! I realized I could apply the insight I gained to other areas of my life. Here I was now, decades later, recalling the lessons of going out on a limb and getting perspective from a different point of view!

- Try climbing a tree, or consider how your life can shift when you venture out on a limb and look at a problem from a higher perspective.

- When you are feeling stuck, repeat the phrase "When you change the way you look at things, the things you look at change." Then consider how you might change the way you are thinking.

- Keep a top-of-mind awareness of the benefits of shifting your perspective.

> We can complain because rose bushes have thorns, or rejoice because thorn bushes have roses.
>
> —ABRAHAM LINCOLN

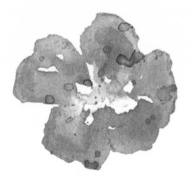

chapter twenty-nine

Move Beyond Your Comfort Zone

This directive has been a personal challenge for me, because I've had to learn to move *far* beyond my comfort zone while creating this new life. As I've said many times, being an artist/entrepreneur is one of the most difficult things I've ever done. I had no idea I'd be so challenged, and yet at the same time, I had no idea that I could accomplish as much as I have. I have been stretched well beyond my comfort zone more times than I'd like to consider. Yet I forge on, stepping into each day learning new things, taking new risks, and exploring new opportunities.

I find it rather ironic that I can write "Life is supposed to be effortless" on one of my inspirational cards. Yet almost in the same breath, the challenges of growing a business from scratch make me wonder, What was I thinking?

I read in a piece of business advice that an entrepreneur must learn to become comfortable with the uncomfortable. So true! I would often repeat the phrase like a mantra, "I'm learning to become comfortable with the uncomfortable," as I was stretching myself into a task or situation where I was clearly out of my comfort zone.

I believe that to be able to grow as a person, in your career, in your relationships, you must stretch yourself beyond the circle of comfort, contentment, and security to that risk-taking, adventurous "courage zone" where growth and opportunity knock and you reap the rewards of opening the door. It's scary, though, and we are not taught or encouraged to go beyond our safety nets in school or society. John F. Kennedy once said, "Nothing worthwhile has ever been accomplished with a guarantee of success." And nothing ever will be. We need to embrace that fact, and instead of fearing the unknown, learn to feel the exhilaration that comes from diving into the unknown. And so what if you make a mistake or experience a setback? With an attitude that everything you do teaches you something, you'll learn to take the nuggets of gold and go on to achieve even greater success. It's all in your attitude and how you define your "setbacks." Put a positive spin on things, make lemonade out of the lemons, and keep moving forward into new and greater possibilities. You'll find that they offer themselves to you as you move beyond your comfort zone.

To sum it up, using the words that I paired with a butterfly on another of my inspirational cards, "I had to give up so much of who I was in order to become who I am now." The message inside the card: "Fly free." If I had not left the comfort of Seattle, my sales position, home, adult children, and friends, I would never have been able to live this life that I only envisioned. It was a big risk, and still is—each day holds opportunities to explore and challenges to overcome. But the trade-off is that I am learning to fly free!

- What will your life be like in 10 years if you stay within your comfort zone? What if, instead, you continually expand your boundaries from the comfort zone to the courage zone?

- Identify the thoughts and fears that hold you back. Commit to looking at them differently and challenging them with new thoughts and viewpoints.

- Today, do something outside your comfort zone. Talk to a stranger in line at the coffee shop, sign up for that class you've always wanted to take, pick up the phone and call the person who can answer a question you've had about starting a new venture.

- When the fear comes up, which it will, take action instead. Lean into the fear and move beyond it.

> Stop being who you were and become who you are.
>
> —PAULO COELHO,
> *The Alchemist*

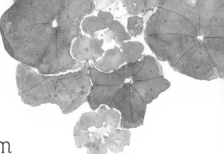

chapter thirty

Practice Random Acts of Kindness

You've seen those bumper stickers, the ones encouraging you to commit "random acts of kindness?" What they can't tell you in that little space is how performing those acts can be a way of transforming yourself. When you begin to focus on extending kindness toward others, you'll feel more kindness coming toward you. Not only will you make someone else's day better, you'll be surprised at how well yours improves.

It's rather like the "secret Santa" gift exchange that many offices and families adopt during the weeks leading up to Christmas. There is delight when you do something for another while keeping your identity a secret. When you watch a person receiving a surprise gift, you see their face change, the eyes open wide with delight, a smile bursting into a grin, and laughter erupting. They appear to feel sheer joy at the unexpected. The old adage is true: "It is in giving that we receive."

The other part of the quote, which is by a San Francisco writer named Anne Herbert, is often left out: "and [practice] senseless acts of beauty." I received a text the other day from a friend who had taken a picture with her phone of a sidewalk outside the coffee shop where she works in San Francisco. Someone had written "It's a beautiful day" with colored chalk on the sidewalk and adorned it with butterflies and hearts. That, to me, is a senseless act of beauty. Think how many people walked on the sidewalk that day and smiled at the childish scrawl reminding them of the beautiful day.

The Hebrew word *mitzvah* means a good deed or an act of kindness. Judaism teaches that the world is built on kindness. I recall what my Bubbe, a dear friend in Salt Lake City who was my son's first caregiver, used to tell me about the importance of doing *mitzvah*s. She believes in the power of doing something good for another person but not telling them about it. She is a perfect example of someone who practices random acts of kindness, and also one who sees and acknowledges the beauty in everyone she meets. I always feel better just by being in her presence.

Entire campaigns focused on practicing random acts of kindness have sprouted up. This, along with "having an attitude of gratitude," enriches my days in many ways. There are myriad ways you can practice random acts of kindness. Don't forget to include yourself when you are doing them!

- Pick up trash you see on the street and make the world a better place.
- Pay for the coffee of the person behind you in line.
- Buy a cookie for a coworker and leave it on their desk.
- Hold the door open for someone.
- Smile at a stranger.
- Send a thank-you note through the mail.
- Take a bubble bath.

When we feel love and kindness toward others, it not only makes others feel loved and cared for, but it helps us also to develop inner happiness and peace.

—THE 14TH DALAI LAMA (1935)

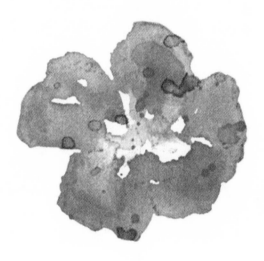

chapter thirty-one

Get a Massage

B ack when I lived in Seattle and my life was completely different, I used to get a massage once a month. For years. It wasn't just a massage; it was an overall body, mind, and soul tune-up. Judith, a gifted healer who became one of my close friends and advisors, worked miracles. Not only could she knead and thaw out my frozen right shoulder each month, she was skilled in traditional Hawaiian lomi lomi massage. From her training, she learned to treat the whole person.

A massage with Judith was really like a therapy session. The intake, prior to the massage, helped identify issues that I might be struggling with both physically and emotionally, and specific zones of the body that might need special attention. Like many healers, Judith views the body in layers. The physical body is overlain by the emotional body, the mental body, and the spiritual body. A healing massage will affect all of these bodies, which combine to create your whole self. When healing occurs on one level, all levels are affected.

I've found that in order to allow my creativity to flow, I need to be open. Energy flows through the body much more easily after blockages are removed. And I can't think of a better way to release the obstructions than a healing message. Lomi lomi is a unique style of massage, derived from the master healers of Hawaii's ancient Polynesian culture. A lomi lomi massage is given in fluid, rhythmic motion, using the forearms as well as the hands. The practitioner works intuitively; a massage may be slow and very relaxing at times, or faster and more invigorating and enlivening to the body. Sometimes the recipient may experience an emotional release: the massage can release negative emotions, beliefs, or memories that were stored in the cells of the body. And the healing effects of the massage can continue long after the massage is over. Any type of massage—Swedish, deep tissue, or hot stone, for example—provides the therapeutic benefits listed below:

- Relieves stress and promotes healing and relaxation
- Improves circulation and lowers blood pressure
- Addresses musculoskeletal issues and improves posture
- Reduces anxiety for a better sense of well-being
- Improves and strengthens the immune system
- Increases body awareness

A massage is the ultimate in pampering. It is a gift to your body, mind, and soul.

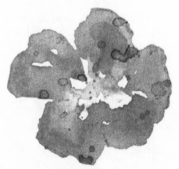

- Book a massage and track how you feel afterward, even a few days after the massage, as your body will continue to release toxins. Make sure to drink plenty of water.

- Have you felt a shift in your energy level? Often I felt exhausted right after a massage, but later would experience an abundance of energy and a flourish of creativity.

The root of all health is in the brain.
The trunk of it is in emotion.
The branches and leaves are the body.
The flower of health blooms
when all parts work together.

—KURDISH FOLK WISDOM

Body and mind and spirit, all combine,
To make the Creature, human and divine.

—ELLA WHEELER WILCOX,
author and poet

chapter thirty-two

101 Things to Do, Be, Have

In 1990, I took a Goal Focusing workshop. One of the exercises involved writing down 101 things that you would like to do, be, or have. I couldn't wait to do this, thinking it would be a piece of cake to come up with 101 things. The instructor had warned us that many people start out gung ho, but at about #50 the writing slows down. She explained that after you commit to paper the obvious ones, like a bigger house, new car, a job you love, it gets harder to come up with ideas. You are stretching yourself beyond the everyday realm of what you think you can do/be/have in your life. You are going to be going out on a limb as you open your mind to new possibilities. And you might find that some resistance comes up. The voice of your inner critic can grow loud in protest as you begin to consider outlandish things.

And that is where the fun of the exercise comes in. As you begin stretching yourself, you'll see yourself doing/being/having things you want without any concern for how they'll show up. Just list them. Here are some examples: riding a bike through the wine country of France; cruising down the Rhine River in Germany; being recognized in your field by winning a prestigious award; living each day with happiness overflowing; owning a condo in your favorite vacation destination; kayaking four times a year; living debt free. You get the picture.

Just for fun, my husband and I took notebooks to the coffee

shop with the intention of creating our own 101 do/be/have lists. I was actually surprised, as we sat there scribbling out ideas, that I wasn't as stumped as I was the first few times I tried it, back in the early 90s. Maybe I'm bubbling over with more creative ideas now. It was interesting, also, to note that Mark's list included many areas around the world he'd like to visit as well as sporting events he'd like to attend, where my list focused on things to do in order to grow my business and creative endeavors I want to accomplish. I do love to dream the impossible dream!

Lou Holtz, the legendary coach of Notre Dame football, is famous for his list of 107 things he wanted to accomplish in his lifetime. He sat down and wrote out the list when he was a married, out-of-work assistant coach whose wife was pregnant with their third child. Only 28 years old at the time, he compiled the list of audacious goals after reading the book *The Magic of Thinking Big*, by David Schwartz, PhD, which his wife had given him to lift his spirits. His inspired list included being invited to dinner at the White House, being on *The Tonight Show*, scoring a hole-in-one, becoming national coach of the year, and leading Notre Dame to a national championship (years before he was ever asked to be the Notre Dame coach). Check, check, check. Over the course of his lifetime he's checked off 102 of the 107 items on the list!

It has been noted repeatedly that the most successful people are those who set goals. And not just any goals: they create a list of all the goals they want to accomplish during their lifetime in several different key life areas, which can include family, finances, travel, charity, vocation, possessions, health, and so on. Keep your list in a place where you can review it. Also feel free to update it with changes. Cross off things you've accomplished and continue to add new items.

As a by-product of the list, you may overcome fears, realize dreams, relish simple pleasures, achieve your goals, and surprise yourself with how much fun you have as you live your ideal, inspired life!

- Get out a piece of paper, grab a pen, and begin writing. See how long it takes till you get to 101 things you would like to do, be, or have.
- Be bold when writing your list.
- What did you learn from this process?
- Did any hidden hopes reveal themselves to you?
- Begin to take the steps necessary to check off items on your list.

> Don't be a spectator, don't let life pass you by.
>
> —LOU HOLTZ,
> Notre Dame Football Coach

chapter thirty-three

Play

P lay. It's quite easy. Really. And it's so much fun to just relax and play! Somehow those two words look funny paired together: relax, then play. Yet I've discovered that when I'm relaxed, I'm much more inclined to be spontaneous and play to my heart's content. *Play* is a word that can describe any number of activities. For instance, we went to play with my cousin and her husband who were in town for the weekend by riding bikes over the Golden Gate Bridge, then on to Sausalito for lunch. I imagined we would stop off and play tourists as we showed off the sights of the city. There was picture taking, story-telling, and laughter. While fully engrossed in play, one is also fully engrossed in the moment. Living in the moment, as we've heard from gurus and guides, is what life is all about!

Sometimes all you need to do to play is not to have any plans, preconceived ideas, or to-do lists to check off. Being spontaneous with a Saturday might be a great introduction to learning to live in the moment and be playful. It's rather like the chicken and the egg. Be spontaneous with your time, and you might decide to do something playful and out of the ordinary—and as a result, you'll be living in the moment and loving life. And if you are playful and living in the moment, you're more apt to be spontaneous as well! Doesn't matter who's on first or what's on second—just have fun and go play!

So envision what you might do on any given Saturday you designate as a play day. We had the best day on our bikes on a Saturday a while back; when we arrived home at the end of the day, we realized that is was the unplanned nature of the day that made it so surprisingly fun. Spontaneity reigned as we rode our bikes to the coffee shop, where we realized it was the first day of racing for the America's Cup, which meant that if we hopped on our bikes and rode down to Marina Green, one of the many viewing areas in San Francisco that are along the waterfront with ample space available for viewing, we'd be able to watch the impressive 72-foot catamarans that would be racing in the bay. We arrived in plenty of time to find a seat at the seawall, along with the many others who came to watch the event. I had my backpack with me, filled with watercolor supplies, and was able to do a *plein air* painting of the sailboats dotting the bay. After we watched the two races, we headed to our last stop, a sports bar, where Mark could check college football scores and we could grab refreshments before heading back home. We kept saying, "Had we planned it, we wouldn't have had as much fun."

When teaching a watercolor class, I always advise students to play with their paints. Somehow the pressure is off for creating the perfect piece of art when I suggest they adopt a playful nature. It frees up the spirit. It loosens one up to experiment. I know from experience that when I'm in a playful mood, I often create a piece of art that I love. It typically feels loose and free rather than forced or overworked, which can happen when I'm trying too hard.

- Designate a play date with a playmate and enjoy what unfolds.

- Play the piano, play with your paints, play charades, checkers, or cards. Play with your kids, play a round of golf, play to your heart's content!

- Play—lighthearted, free, spontaneous, engaged, and truly living in the moment.

Humanity has advanced, when it has advanced, not because it has been sober, responsible, and cautious, but because it has been playful, rebellious, and immature.

—TOM ROBBINS,
Even Cowgirls Get the Blues

chapter thirty-four

Brainstorm

T o really get your creative juices going, have a brainstorming session! Though I always thought of brainstorming as an activity done with others, I've discovered that I can brainstorm with myself just as effectively. So gather your coworkers around the conference table and white board, call up your friends for a fun brainstorming session, or just open up a pad of paper and begin brainstorming on your own.

Brainstorm about an idea you want to explore, brainstorm about where you want to go for vacation, brainstorm about how you see your life unfolding over the next year, brainstorm about a project you've been putting off, brainstorm for clarity about any situation that has you perplexed. You can take any topic and start the process.

I have discovered that when I open up a notepad to a blank page and start writing with the intention of brainstorming, it's almost as if I can feel the crown of my head opening up and inspiration pouring through. I start writing so fast, trying to capture all the ideas. A year ago I was struggling with the direction of my business. Ideas and thoughts had been swirling around my head while I was walking around overwhelmed and confused. One day I grabbed a large newsprint pad and my colored markers and began brainstorming. I wrote a question at the top of the page, and then the answers began to flow. With the attitude that nothing you write is wrong when brainstorming, I found myself writing outlandish ideas, and not only writing, but drawing. I kept at it—and six pages later I had found clarity about the direction of the business. Rather than thinking that things had to be only one way, I realized that I could work on both trying to find licensing opportunities for my art and developing my own line of paper products. It was a revelation for me. By the end of that session, I felt spent, and drew a picture of a body lying horizontally. I needed to go lie down and take a nap! I believe the nap helped me integrate all that I had discovered. (See chapter 44 for more about naps.)

Another brainstorming session I held with myself was on a flight home to Indiana last year. I had been communicating with someone who licenses art for calendars at a publisher in Indianapolis. Going home for my nephew's wedding seemed like the perfect opportunity to meet with her in person. It was my persistence that allowed me to get the appointment in the first place. I had been told that although they liked my artwork, they really didn't need another inspirational watercolor calendar. So I knew, in order for them to consider another calendar, I'd have to come up with a different theme as the subject. I opened up my notebook and began moving my pen, writing the obvious: "I need to come up with an idea." The scribbling continued, then it stopped once I had written "Challenge yourself." That's it! I love to challenge myself—for years I've created a birthday-month challenge: every September I challenge myself to do one activity on every day of the month, which I mentioned in chapter 25.

It all began when my doctor suggested I walk every day. I was so impressed with myself for completing that consistent daily practice that I challenged myself to paint for a specified time (a half hour or an hour). When I saw that I had written "Challenge yourself" on the plane, I knew I was on to something. I began writing in earnest, fast and furious—so many ideas were floating into my head, I was trying to capture them all before they escaped me. By the time I was done, I had scripted out an idea for the "creativity challenge" calendar that offered a challenge for each month of the year. January was "Brainstorm Your Best Life for the Year." May was "Creating a Collage or Writing/Drawing Your Vision." For December, the "Season of Lights," I suggested lighting a candle each evening, saying a prayer for someone who needs blessings. I had so much fun on the plane that day, and the brainstorming session with myself produced amazing results. My excitement was contagious: I was asked to write up a formal submission. Brainstorming—it works! Try it and see:

- Find a large piece of paper (newsprint pads are available at office supply and art stores), and write down your question or the problem for which you are seeking a solution.

- Tape the paper on the wall and start throwing out ideas, writing them down no matter how outlandish they sound.

- After a set amount of time, stop and review what you've produced.

- Cull the best ideas, so you can begin to explore those in greater detail.

- Have fun with the process!

> It is easier to tone down a wild idea
> than to think up a new one.
>
> —ALEX OSBORN,
> advertising executive, father of brainstorming

chapter thirty-five

Read with Your Ears

We learn from books, we are entertained by them, and we can be inspired by their ideas. But who's to say we have to actually *read* a book? We can *listen* to a book as well. I have a friend, John, who used to endure quite a grueling commute each day that had him driving nearly an hour each way. He did this for many years. How did he endure the drive? By listening to books on tape. John swore by them. He listened to the classics, to new books, to all sorts of books. It was always entertaining to get in his car and hear what he was reading!

I'm a voracious reader—at any time I might be reading a few books simultaneously. The table next to my bed is always overflowing with books. A few are typically inspirational in nature, others biographical and then there is always the entertaining novel that can hold me captive for hours at a time. What better way to keep reading during the day than to listen to a book?

Google, my knowledgeable friend, provided a "Top 10 Educational Benefits of Audiobook Listening" list written with teens in mind (by Pam Spence Holley). After I read through it, I felt anyone would benefit from listening to audiobooks, no matter what their age. Here's the list:

10. Removes any stigma of lower reading levels or "uncool" genres

9. Increases vocabulary skills

8. Improves speaking and writing skills

7. Introduces storytelling, an important tradition in human history

6. Engages imagination by allowing students to create mental images of the story

5. Improves listening skills—essential in this multi-media world

4. Makes mundane yet necessary tasks (exercising, dishwashing, room cleaning) more tolerable

3. Keeps students informed of popular books or latest releases from favorite authors

2. Improves ability to multitask and complete assignments simultaneously

1. Listening is an important step for becoming a lifelong reader

After reading through this list, I felt #8 was the best benefit, until I looked closer and chose #5. But I wasn't satisfied with that choice, because I thought introducing storytelling, #7, was a good thing. By the time I was finished, I decided that #6 was the winner. Anything that engages our imagination is truly a benefit, because imagination allows you to create the life you choose!

Just recently, I began listening to an audiobook. I have not made a practice out of listening to books on tape, but I'm reconsidering; I have really enjoyed listening and learning as I drive. I've been thinking about John and how he used to pick up his books on tape at the public library. When was the last time you went to your neighborhood library? I recently attended an open house for the new library in our neighborhood. I was amazed at all the tools, programs, and activities the library had to offer. Clearly, it can be a resource for the community as well as for you.

- Go check out your local library, then check out an audiobook!

- The next time you know you'll be spending a long period of time in your car, find an audio book that interests you that you can listen to as you drive.

- Complete a book report by telling someone about a recent book you listened to rather than read, and why you enjoyed the process.

I guess my guilty pleasure would be listening to the British audio versions of the "Harry Potter" books.

—DAVID SEDARIS,
Me Talk Pretty One Day

chapter thirty-six

Try On Something New

Y ou most likely think of clothes when you think of trying on something new—at least I do. That is not a bad place to start: it can be a metaphor for trying on new experiences, new thoughts, a new outlook on life, a new way of looking at the world.

One of the most formative books for me was *You Can Heal Your Life*, by Louise Hay. I discovered it years ago, and Hay's concept of changing your life by simply changing your thinking was profound for me when I first encountered it. It's really so simple. To change, you only have to be willing to change your thinking about something. In other words, try looking at it from a different viewpoint. When you try on a new thought, you are opening yourself up to the likelihood that you can change your old behavior and old beliefs about how the world works, and therefore begin anew.

About five years ago, I lost 30 pounds, thanks to Weight Watchers and my husband, who asked me to attend meetings with him. I had no clue when we started the program that I'd drop three dress sizes and 30 pounds. But I did. I also tried on lots of new clothes during that seven-month period while my body was shedding weight. The really intriguing part of the process, for me, was the fact that not only did I lose weight, but I also dropped a lot of ideas about who I was and embraced new ideas about how I might live my life.

What was really profound, as I realized later and was explaining to friends, was that when I lost all that weight, I also lost 19 years of weight (or stuff) that I had crammed into the various nooks, crannies, closets and basement of my home in West Seattle. It was by no means an easy project to prepare my old home for sale—the home that I had lived in and loved for so many years. And just like losing the weight off my bones, it took about seven months to do the actual work needed to transform the bones of my old home to its new glory. The old house tried on a lot of "something new": a new sidewalk leading up to the front porch, new wood flooring on the front porch, new paint throughout the downstairs, a new mailbox, new shrubs and flowers.

I didn't recognize, at the time, that I was changing much more than my physical body. Yet my physical body led the entire transformation process that was beginning to unfold for me. Since our physical body and the clothes we wear announce who we are to the world, it is only fitting that by trying on something new, we are willing to announce that there is something new about to be birthed within us—or that we are looking to reveal different parts of ourselves or discover hidden talents. Are you willing to try on new styles? Are you willing to try wearing colors instead of the basic black? How about trying a different hairdo or different color of lipstick? There are so many minor modifications we can make to our appearance that might make a major difference in how we view ourselves.

Trying on something new can expand to trying yoga instead of Pilates, or taking a new route for a walk. You'll discover new scenery. Try riding a bike rather than running or walking for your exercise. Instead of watching TV, try reading a book for half an hour. Try a new restaurant, or when you go to your favorite restaurant, try something new—maybe one of the daily specials. One of the new things we changed was purchasing low-fat sour cream rather than regular. At first my husband balked, but then he realized he couldn't taste the difference! It's so easy to make the minor modifications that can lead to much bigger changes. Try it and see. Record your changes in your journal. Start small.

- Try on new clothes (the obvious).
- Try taking a different route to work.
- Work your way up to trying out different ways of looking at the world.

> If you want to succeed you should strike out on new paths, rather than travel the worn paths of accepted success.
>
> —JOHN D. ROCKEFELLER,
> American industrialist and philanthropist

chapter thirty-seven
Read, Run, Write, Draw

Those four words were my mantra back when I was in college. My goal then was to have the time and the freedom each day to read, write, run, and draw. I've been out of college for 30+ years and have yet to successfully complete all four activities on a consistent daily basis. However, I can say that over that 30-year period, those four activities have always inspired me. They were and still are my passions in life. These passions motivated me to take classes, to run 10K races and a few half marathons, to keep countless journals filled with writings, drawings, and paintings of daily life, and to read books, both fiction and nonfiction, on many interesting subjects. But most of all, those four words that defined my avocations became my vocation. Words and Watercolors was born out of my love for creating inspired words with watercolor images to share with my friends and family. Looking back, I can see that my interests were my future pulling me forward into this creative life I'm now lucky enough to live today.

It can be said that working on your passions, interests, or hobbies—call them what you will—can provide many benefits for your health and well-being. Listed below are a few of the benefits:

- Having hobbies allows you to be connected to others through activities as diverse as knitting circles, golf foursomes, and creative writing groups. You develop a network of friends and can have fun as you share your interest.

- Pursuing your passion brings joy into your life through the pleasure of engaging in an activity that delights you.

- Hobbies provide relaxation in a positive form and can assist in stress reduction.

Recently I've been learning about the quilting world, because my artwork has been licensed for a collection of quilting fabric. It's been a real eye-opener to see how passionate people are for fabric and quilting and all that goes with it. There are sewing machines to purchase and any number of fabrics, trim, and patterns to discover. It's an activity that can be shared with family, friends, and loved ones. Passed down from generation to generation are not only the quilts, but also the love of the practice of quilting. A woman who owned a quilt fabric store told me recently that more money is spent annually on quilting than on golf. I was shocked! Having talked to many quilters recently, I can see that their creativity is unleashed as they work with the fabric; I call them artists whose medium is fabric, as opposed to paint, words, ceramics, or theater.

- What activities have inspired you over the years?
- Do you still make time to develop your passions?
- Have you become proficient at any one activity?
- What are your hobbies?
- How do you spend your leisure time?

I hope these questions will motivate you to consider the activities that make you happy. What inspires you? Once you identify that, I hope you can make a committed effort to exploring it fully.

> Today is life—the only life you are sure of. Make the most of today. Get interested in something. Shake yourself awake. Develop a hobby. Let the winds of enthusiasm sweep through you. Live today with gusto.
>
> —DALE CARNEGIE,
> *How to Win Friends and Influence People*

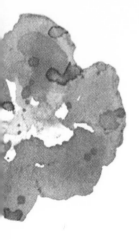

chapter thirty-eight
Look for
"Meant to Be's"

T hings happen in your life that may not make sense at the
time, but when you look back on them you can say, "Oh,
that was meant to be!" Like my friendship with Eve,
which began when I was a carpet queen and used to travel to
Portland, Oregon, for work. I called on Eve, who at the time was
the supervisor for facilities planning for PGE (Portland General
Electric). We became friends over the course of many sales calls
and lunches, to the point where I became a regular at Eve's home
for dinner when I traveled to Portland.

One day Eve's mom, Ardis, asked Eve if she knew any artists,
because she was looking for someone to paint a cover for the
book she was self-publishing, *Facing Age: Finding Answers*.
Ardis had an idea of what she wanted: something botanical. Eve,
who had been a recipient of my calendar titled "In the Garden,"
knew I had a talent for painting flowers. It just so happened that
I was in town that day, so Eve invited me to dinner to meet her
mom. As Ardis and I talked, we kept laughing because it all
seemed so "meant to be." We shared a zest for living, a curiosity
about life, and an interest in helping people.

Ardis had been a journalist, among many other careers, and
still wrote a weekly column for the local paper, the *Lake Oswego
Review*. Many of her columns focused on what she was learning
about the aging process. She had questions about the particu-

lars of dealing with numerous practical matters: everything from how to know when you should stop driving, to how to choose a retirement center, to what documents need to be assembled for power of attorney. She was doing the research for herself but knew that others would benefit, which led to the idea of turning her weekly columns into a book. I was honored that she considered my art for the cover.

I selected climbing clematis as the subject for the painting. The finished high-resolution scan of my artwork was submitted to her printer, but for reasons still not clear to either of us, they didn't want to use it. Even though I was disappointed, I was able to turn that lovely clematis into a greeting card once I began my own card line a few years later. Ardis and I agreed that it was meant to be. We would constantly find coincidences that seemed meant to be and we would laugh and laugh each time we met and discovered more "meant to be's."

It became a theme through Eve's family—looking for things that seemed meant to be. Eve herself had an experience that was meant to be: The facility planning manager at Nike, Pat, needed to find a replacement for herself. She was looking for someone with her own varied and broad-based skills, which were required for the position. Having known Eve for many years, Pat called and suggested Eve apply for the job. Eve wasn't looking to leave PGE, but knowing it's always good to keep your options open, thought it might be fun to see what would happen if she applied. She'd been impressed with Nike when she worked there as a temp 20 years earlier and thought, What do I have to lose? She applied and, lo and behold, got the position. It was clearly a career move that seemed meant to be. Eve was rewarded with a much more exciting, vibrant, exhilarating atmosphere to walk into each day.

Eve's husband, Paul, also had his own "meant to be" experience about that time. He's now enjoying success with his own company, Innovative Nightscapes—a success that began when his former employer, a landscape contractor, asked him to be in charge of the landscape lighting for the company. What he discovered was an entire industry that captivated him. He realized he'd found his passion when a customer shared with him that she would drag her lawn chair into her backyard and stare up into her trees for hours after the sky had turned to night and the lights lit up her trees in such a fashion that it looked like a piece of art. He was hooked, knowing that he could bring beauty into people's yards with innovative lighting that illuminated their landscapes. He felt it was meant to be: the pull to leave the comfort of his job and strike out on his own as a contractor.

It's only fitting that I started this chapter as I sat on the back deck at Eve and Paul's on a perfect summer evening in the Pacific Northwest. It's now years later, but our friendship has remained intact. This is the third summer that I've traveled up to Portland in August to attend the Far West Nursery Trade Show. It's the perfect venue for meeting garden centers and nurseries that are potential accounts for my Words and Watercolors line of cards and gifts. It was meant to be when Eve and I met many years ago and became friends. Who knew how our respective lives would shift and change as time passed? But we've been there to watch and support each other—and it's always felt meant to be!

- Be on the lookout for your own "meant to be" situations.

- Write them down and pledge to be conscious as you go about your daily routines.

- Looking back over your life, see how a "meant to be" situation occurred and changed your view of the world.

I look at things as "Everything is meant to be."

—LIL WAYNE,
rapper

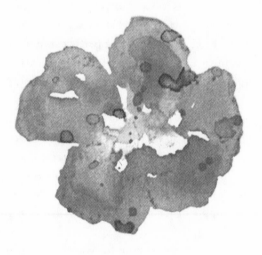

152

chapter thirty-nine

Look Up at the Moon

I t's appropriate that I began writing this chapter on the evening of a new moon. I have been intrigued with the power of the moon from the time I was young. As a waitress in college, I worked at a rather upscale restaurant. On evenings when everything seemed to go wrong or there were more crazy customers than usual, someone would usually ask, "Is there a full moon tonight?" It was those crazy evenings when I first made the connection between the full moon and erratic behavior. I discovered that the word *lunatic* originated from the Latin word *luna*, for moon. The fact that the cycles of the moon could cause temporary insanity was an idea that I found fascinating.

The moon revolves continuously around the earth. As it does so, its appearance changes. The cycle begins at a new moon, where the moon is invisible, and moves through the first quarter (crescent-shaped), full moon, third quarter (another crescent shape but opposite the first-quarter shape), and back to new. Just look up at the sky at night; once you spot the moon, you can determine what phase it is in by the shape. What a great way to connect with your moon goddess!

The moon, in all her glory and power, represents the goddess, the female principal, our intuitive nature, our dreams and unconscious. She is a sight to behold at whatever phase, and if asked, I believe, can provide assistance to your daily life. One early morning when out on my daily jog, many years ago when I was living in Seattle, I went down to Lowman Beach, which faces Puget Sound. I can still recall the peaceful stillness that enveloped me as I sat on a driftwood log watching the full moon setting in the west. Though her brilliant light was waning as daylight emerged, I asked her to fill me with her "moonbeams, moon dust, and moon magic" as I went about my day. I loved the sound of that prayer and jotted it down in my journal when I returned home. Years later I paired those words with an image of the full moon rising and it became one of my inspirational cards. I wanted others to see the words and tap into the power that she can bestow through her benevolent nature.

The new moon is the time when you can reset your intentions for the coming month. The darkness of the new moon reminds us that this is the time when the old passes away and the new is not yet here. It is the still point. That is why it is a powerful time for sending out your prayers, wishes, and desires to the Universe. What do you want to bring into your life? Dream big. The moon will be expanding, and inspired with her magic, you just might be surprised at how your goals and intentions manifest in the light of the full moon! During the full moon, you will begin to make out the path, see the possibilities begin to unfold, take a step forward into the dreams you seeded earlier. It is both a culmination and a time to act on something you imagined. The full moon is filled with magic. Don't be afraid to tap into it!

So how can noticing the phases of the moon make a difference in your life today? Working with the energies of the new and full moon can bring an entirely new awareness into your life. Just connecting to another heavenly body can open you to the power of the divine. Try it!

- Look up and find the moon in the sky tonight. Consider asking your goddess energy for help with any issue you may have and then watch and listen for her subtle answers.
- Keep track of the phases of the moon for a few months.

I have gazed at, painted, sketched, and photographed full moons, crescent moons, and waxing moons. I've talked to the moon, asked her for guidance, rejoiced at her beauty, and always have been in awe of her presence. I hope you enjoy discovering her power and beauty as much as I have over the years.

> Shoot for the moon and if you miss you will still be among the stars.
>
> —LES BROWN,
> motivational speaker

chapter forty

Make Your
Own Mantra

M any people are familiar with the Serenity Prayer: "God grant me the serenity to accept the things I cannot change; courage to change the things I can; and wisdom to know the difference." There is power in repeating a phrase that offers a touchstone for peace. I have recited the Serenity Prayer many times over the years. It has literally saved my sanity when I've been obsessing or worrying about something I cannot control. It reminds me to "let Go and let God," another one of my favorite mantras.

What is a mantra, you ask? A mantra is a sound, syllable, word, or phrase that is considered capable of creating transformation. Its use and type varies according to the school and philosophy associated with the mantra. Mantras are traditionally syllables and poems in the Sanskrit language created through a complex numerical system based on the date and time of your birth as well as the numeric value of your name. Today, mantras are more widely understood as any statement that affirms the way we want to live our lives.

The syllable *Om* is the most basic mantra. It is believed to be the sound of the Universe. Chanting *Om* marks the beginning and the end of the yoga class I attend. It is a vibration that can be felt in the chest. I feel the peace descend into my body as I hold my hands in prayer position in front of my heart and utter, "Om." It is a centering practice.

How do you find your own mantra? It can be as easy as Googling "mantras," but most likely you are already familiar with some and use them unconsciously. What words or phrases do you repeat over and over to yourself? Listen closely to the way you talk to yourself, and if it is not in a loving, kind way, you may want to consider repeating some positive affirmations that will invite transformation into your life at a subtle level.

Another way to work with your mantra is to carry it around in your pocket. I love those little stones you can buy that have words etched in them: dream, inspire, beauty, peace, believe, create, love, possibility. They're rather like the do-it-yourself poetry words you can purchase for your refrigerator door. Collect stones with words on them and place them next to your computer or on your desk. Play with the words on your refrigerator. Write various mantras in your journal, and begin to repeat them for a day or two. As you discover the power in a mantra, record how it changes you. Are your thoughts different? Are you able to switch from negative thinking to positive?

Play around with words. Have fun with them. Learn what a useful tool words can be in offering a way to change aspects of your life. I've found that when I engage a mantra and say it often, it becomes like a prayer. The peace and serenity that I'm repeating in my prayer actually descend, and I begin to feel calmer.

Here are a few mantras you can try:

- "I keep my head up and my heart open."
- "Be the change you wish to see in the world." (Gandhi)
- "Love is the only miracle there is." (Osho)
- Create your own mantra. Here's one: "Each moment I vibrate love to all."

> I change my thoughts, I change my world.
>
> —NORMAN VINCENT PEALE,
> *The Power of Positive Thinking*

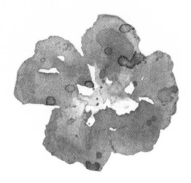

chapter forty-one

Create a Circle

F orm a circle, or gathering, of people who come together for a specific purpose on a regular basis. It could be women only, or men only, or both sexes. Many years ago in Seattle I joined a shaman circle. At that time, I really didn't have a clue what a sacred circle was, let alone a shaman circle, but circumstances conspired for me to meet Christine, who would become my shaman teacher. Christine, an amazing person, brought together a diverse group of women into her circle with the intention of teaching us about the shaman/Native American world. As coincidences usually go, I thought it was significant that just prior to meeting Christine, books about Native American culture were practically falling into my lap. It would become my area of interest for the next few years. Our shaman circle met every two weeks on Wednesday evenings. Friendships were formed and a lot of healing occurred as we learned to trust our instincts, be open to the way nature communicates with us, and look to our spirit guides or plant guides for guidance. (See the end of this chapter for book recommendations.)

It didn't happen overnight, but I did create a shaman circle, with the help of my friends Michaela and Lauren, after moving to San Francisco. It had been nearly four years since I was part of a regular circle when the three of us began journeying together every two weeks. Now there are five of us: Michaela invited two of her friends she met working at the Reiki clinic. Gifted healers all, we spend time connecting, telling stories about our lives, sharing about specific issues confronting us, and then doing a "journey." A journey in the shaman tradition is similar to doing a meditation. Entering an altered state of mind, one communicates and interacts with the spiritual realms. I feel so honored and blessed to have found a very supportive group of women to be witness to my process in life. That's what a circle can do for you: provide friendship, support, advice, and encouragement for your journey through the trials and tribulations of life.

You can create a circle with any group that gets together on a regular basis. Whether the focus is on food (gourmet club), reading (book club), connecting (networking groups), or crafting (quilters guilds, knitting groups), a circle allows you to form bonds and share life, creativity, interests, and enjoyment. As a bonus, you'll develop a whole new circle of friends as well!

- Find a shaman circle to explore.

- Ask some friends to join you in your circle of interest.

- Decide on a regular time to meet and the focus of your circle.

A few of the books that fell into my lap:

- *Winona's Web: A Novel of Discovery*, by Priscilla Cogan

- *Coyote Medicine: Lessons from Native American Healing*, by Lewis Mehl-Madrona MD

- *Medicinemaker: Mystic Encounters on the Shaman's Path*, by Hank Wesselman

A few of the books that introduced me to the shaman world

- *Shamanic Journeying: A Beginner's Guide*, by Sandra Ingerman
- *Shaman, Healer, Sage: How to Heal Yourself and Others with the Energy Medicine of the Americas*, by Alberto Villoldo PhD
- *Animal Speak: The Spiritual & Magical Powers of Creatures Great & Small*, by Ted Andrews

> Wherever possible, create a circle where people can safely share deep experience and diverse viewpoints. There are many circle formats, but their one central concept is to demonstrate reverence for the truth of another person's experience.
>
> —JAMES O'DEA,
> *Cultivating Peace*

chapter forty-two

Honor the Changing of Seasons

My favorite time of year, the solstice! It will be here in a couple of days and I've been so busy that I haven't spread the word about my annual Summer Solstice party. However, I know that those who made it to the Winter Solstice party will be in attendance for another ritual celebrating the rotation of the earth and the changing of the seasons.

My fascination with the solstice began many years ago when a friend invited me to a Winter Solstice party on Vashon Island, an island near Seattle with a population of 11,000 residents. I took the ferry, a 15-minute ride from West Seattle, and met up with my friends Steve and Terry at their home before heading over to their friends Jeff and Marla's place. It was the longest night of the year, and we were going to be celebrating the Winter Solstice and the return of the sun. Jeff, who worked in construction, always built a huge bonfire for the celebration. The stack of wood towered over 12 feet tall, with a girth of about six feet. Very impressive!

It was such a contrast to go from the dark, cold night into the warmth of their festive home. Neighbors welcomed each other, exchanging holiday greetings, consuming wine and food, everyone partaking of the table laden with goodies. Marla handed out pencils and paper to everyone, encouraging us to write down on one sheet what we wanted to release from the old year and on another what we wanted to pull in for the New Year. I asked if I could have more than one piece of paper. Yes! The conversation stopped, the pencils busy capturing thoughts. Grabbing our hats, coats, and gloves with papers in hand, we made our way outside, forming a circle around the bonfire, which was beginning to roar to life. It was a perfect night. A midnight-blue sky was studded with stars and the cold, crisp air allowed you to see your breath. Everyone held hands and began singing songs to Great Spirit as we gave thanks for the light returning. All of a sudden a bright orb began to shine through the bonfire. The light of the sun returns! We began the rounds of releasing the old and pulling in the new as we threw our papers onto the fire. The sparks of paper flamed up to the sky, carrying our hopes and dreams upward where Great Spirit could read them.

I was captivated with the magic of that evening. From then on, I celebrated my own Winter Solstice with a party each year, though mine was a bit modified. I didn't have it on the exact day of the solstice; I celebrated on the Saturday before Christmas, combining a traditional holiday party with my solstice party. Instead of a huge bonfire, I would shepherd everyone out to my patio, where a large grill provided the fire that transformed the Post-It notes with our hopes and dreams written on them into sparks that flew up to the heavens. Even without the drama of a bonfire, I heard many times over the years how powerful the ritual was for my friends. People shared how, months later, they realized that what they had written and thrown into the fire had come to pass. I believe it has something to do with setting an intention and then letting it go. That's where the magic happens!

After many years of holding a Winter Solstice party, I decided to throw a Summer Solstice party. I wasn't sure what the ritual should be, so after considerable research, I came up with the idea of having a "boasting and toasting" party. Appropriately, we would celebrate the fullness of the sun/longest day of the year by boasting and toasting of the fullness of our accomplishments. The first six months of the year had passed, and it was time to observe our achievements, successes, and proud moments. The grill was pressed into service once again to grill hamburgers and hot dogs for the summer kickoff party. After everyone had eaten and just as the sun was beginning to set in the night sky, we once again stoked the fire by throwing the wreath from the previous Christmas onto the grill. After six months of hanging on the back porch, it was dry and brittle—it flared up fast and furious, the evergreen fragrance from the pine boughs wafting in the air. Champagne was uncorked, bubbly was poured, and the sharing began as everyone gathered around the grill "boasting and toasting."

- Create a ritual of your own to honor the changing of the seasons.

- Consider how noting your achievements makes you feel inspired and confident.

- Release something from the old year and call in something new you are looking forward to in the New Year.

In the depth of winter, I finally learned that within me there lay an invincible summer.

—ALBERT CAMUS,
The Stranger

chapter forty-three

Visit a Museum

Along with many other creative types, I was a big fan of Julia Cameron's book *The Artist's Way*, when it first came out in the 90s. A dedicated disciple, for a while at least, I completed her suggested "morning pages," writing for three pages each morning without fail, in longhand (no computer), anything that popped into my head: a stream of consciousness flow, a way to wake up, get clarity on the day, and clear out the cobwebs of my mind. I also enjoyed her idea of "artist's dates," a weekly solo expedition to explore something that interests you—it might be taking your sketchbook outside and drawing, watching the sunset, taking a walk and noticing anything that catches your eye, or opening a box of 64 Crayolas and a coloring book. The concept of playing with your creativity opens you up to exploring and expanding your view of the world, which results in enhanced or recharged creativity. In the spirit of artist's dates, I offer the suggestion to visit a museum.

In Los Angeles for a wedding recently, we visited the Getty Villa. The grandeur of the complex alone is awe-inspiring, not to mention the treasures within. As we exited from the parking garage, a docent greeted us. Interesting and entertaining, he whetted our appetites with a few tidbits of history regarding the center and J. Paul Getty, the man behind this replica of the Villa dei Papiri, a Roman country house in Herculaneum buried by the eruption of Mount Vesuvius in AD 79. We descended the stairs of the outdoor amphitheater, and as I turned around to look back, I marveled at the incredible design details. The handrail was exquisite and the terraced landscape to the side of the seating was nothing short of lovely. I couldn't wait to enter.

We began with a 12-minute film about the collection of Greek and Roman antiquities started by J. Paul Getty; the architecture that inspired the design of the Villa; and the ongoing work to preserve the antiquities. It helped to get a bit of history and sense of place before ambling through the various rooms, which held collections that showcased amazing statues from the Etruscans, Greeks, and Romans. On the walls and floors there were silver treasures and bronze vessels; terra-cotta and marble sarcophagi lined the walls. I was impressed with the stories that accompanied the displays. My favorite room was called "Gods and Goddesses," where I was reminded of the power that gods held over life at that time. I decided I'd do a bit more research on various gods and goddesses myself and incorporate some prayers to those with whom I felt a connection. A terra-cotta relief of the Muses who inspire writing made me recognize that I needed to find my own literary muse to assist me with this book!

We walked out to the gardens and immediately I was struck, once again, by beauty everywhere. A fountain stood in the middle of the garden; water erupted from the mouths of brass animal heads and bubbled over to the water lilies and grasses below. I began clicking away on my camera, trying to frame the perfect artistic photo. Then I looked up and saw a wall fountain made from the most vivid mosaic colors and seashells—it literally took my breath away. Click, click, click: I tried to capture the magnificence of this replica of the ancient fountain in the House of the Large Fountain at Pompeii. This was in the East Garden; we still had the Outer Peristyle to discover, comprising formal gardens that offered a peaceful place for conversation and contemplation.

We sat down for a minute, and I tried to breathe in the beauty all around me. I knew that somehow I would be taking this calm, serene setting with me when I left. We sat below a grape arbor. Click, click, click. I was intrigued with the winding vines, large leaves, and clusters of green grapes. If only I could have set up shop and painted right there. I did have my backpack with travel watercolors, but we didn't have the time it would take for me to even begin a sketch. I'd have to settle for digital images.

A museum doesn't have to feature art. A few years ago, Mark and I visited the San Francisco Fire Department Museum, a treasure trove of old photographs, maps of the city, and recorded stories about the big fire that resulted from the 1906 earthquake. It was the perfect thing to do on a cool, rainy, winter Sunday afternoon.

- Take yourself out to a museum and soak in the knowledge waiting to be shared.

- Is there a museum you've thought of visiting? Don't put it off any longer. Make plans to check it out.

- Take your sketchbook with you; when inspired, stop and draw!

> I maintain that if you're a novelist and you go into an art museum, you'll come out a better novelist. And if you paint a picture for an hour you're a better actor at the end of it.
>
> —JOHN HAWKES,
> film and television actor

chapter forty-four
Take a Nap

I'm writing this while still in that dreamy world between naptime and real time. I love a nap in the middle of the day. As far as I'm concerned, there's nothing better for restoring yourself than taking a siesta. I was up early this morning, meditated, did email, labored a bit with words, and by 8:30 a.m. I was ready to jump on my bike. My husband and I had a scenic morning ride along the waterfront and then up through town. We got to our usual coffee shop, read the paper, then back on the bikes to Golden Gate Park, where I sat in the sun and sketched in my journal while Mark caught up with his sister on the phone. After preparing a late lunch back home, we were both a bit tired from the activity, sunshine, and exercise. A nap was clearly in order. Without feeling a bit guilty, I got into bed and quickly fell into a good sleep. Upon awakening slowly, I thought of this chapter that I wanted to write and fired up the computer.

I began typing away and then remembered one of the favorite books I read to my children when they were little. I went to the bookshelves and found it, *The Napping House*, by Audrey Wood, illustrated by Don Wood. It's a charming, rhyming tale of a family where everyone is snoozing until—the surprise! It was a favorite in our house when the kids were young and we had our own version of "the napping family" on weekend afternoons. My son, Bob, never hesitated to take a nap, and he often announced, "I go na-ne now" when he was ready for a nap. "Na-ne" became one of those words in our family vocabulary that continues to this day.

Naps can be a powerful tool for self-improvement. They can increase not only our health and well-being but our intelligence and productivity. There are many benefits to napping. Among them:

- Increasing alertness. The National Sleep Foundation recommends a short nap of 20–30 minutes "for improved alertness and performance without leaving you feeling groggy or interfering with night-time sleep."

- Preventing burnout. In our Western culture with its highly regarded work ethic, we are constantly on the go. Taking a nap relieves stress and provides a fresh start to the rest of your day. It's like a system reboot!

- Heightening sensory perception and creativity. According to Dr. Sara C. Mednick, author of *Take a Nap!: Change Your Life*, napping can restore the sensitivity of your sight, hearing, and taste. It also improves creativity by relaxing your mind and allowing new associations to form.

- Improving health. A Harvard study found that those who took a midday siesta at least three times a week are 37 percent less likely to die of heart disease.

- Increasing productivity. Numerous studies show that workers become increasingly unproductive as the day wears on, but another Harvard study demonstrated that a 30-minute nap boosted the performance of workers, restoring their productivity to beginning-of-the-day levels.

You have good company if you take naps. We have all heard stories about Edison and Einstein and their prolific discoveries. Both were famous nappers as well. Did their naps increase their creativity? Add to the list presidents John F. Kennedy and Ronald Reagan. I was happy to see a woman, Eleanor Roosevelt, make the list of nappers; she was known to nap before giving speeches. Another politician who was famous for naps was Winston Churchill. Here is his take on naps:

> *"You must sleep some time between lunch and dinner, and no half-way measures. Take off your clothes and get into bed. That's what I always do. Don't think you will be doing less work because you sleep during the day. That's a foolish notion held by people who have no imagination. You will be able to accomplish more. You get two days in one—well, at least one and a half, I'm sure. When the war started, I had to sleep during the day because that was the only way I could cope with my responsibilities."*

I have to admit that I agree with Churchill. I do get a lot more accomplished on those days when I succumb to an afternoon nap. When I join my cats on the couch for a bit of shut-eye, I typically have more energy to work into the evening on the projects I have going. So I'll keep taking my naps, and I hope you will too!

- Indulge in an afternoon siesta, and note how you feel later in the day.
- If you have young children, take a nap when they do.

> Learn from yesterday, live for today, look to tomorrow, rest this afternoon.
>
> —CHARLES M. SCHULZ,
> *Charlie Brown's Little Book of Wisdom*

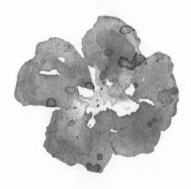

chapter forty-five

Keep Track of Your Dreams

There are the dreams we dream each night and there are the dreams that we envision each day. The daydreams give us a vision and provide hope for a better life. They often encourage us to make the changes necessary to lead us to where we want to be. The nighttime dreams are another story. They can be our unconscious talking to us—our soul speaking up, knocking at the door of our consciousness. They can be crystal clear about the action we need to take, or they can be played out in the rich imagery of the metaphorical world. I believe both night and day dreams are important to creating a rich life. Both call for a journal nearby so you can easily grab a pen and record the insights and messages that come on the wings of dreams.

I have long been fascinated with dreams, most likely a result of having precognitive dreams when I was in my early 20s. Back then, there was not the proliferation of information so readily available as there is today with the Internet, where any subject can be researched in depth. I recall going to the local library, looking up "dreams" in the card catalog, and searching for the few books on that topic. This was my first foray into the land of dreams. I learned about precognitive dreams, or dreams that convey some knowledge in advance, from a book in the library. Such dreams are not uncommon; many people get answers to questions or warnings of future events in their dreams.

I also think it is important to share the power of dreams with your children. My kids and I always shared our dreams over cereal at the breakfast table. It was no surprise to me when they both had precognitive dreams of their own. Bob and Emily were comfortable talking about their dreams, as they had grown up with the idea of dreams being a part of life. They knew that dreams can provide a different way to access information and knowing. We often laughed, though, at the dreams Emily would make up just so she'd have something to say. She was about seven years old and didn't want to be left out of the discussion!

Starting a dream journal can offer valuable insight into your world. Keep your dream journal nearby. It's best to capture your dreams just as you are waking up, when the dream world is still with you. I've found that if I don't capture the dream immediately, it fades quickly in the light of day. Remember, too, that the unconscious often speaks in metaphors. That is why you may need some time to sit with the dream so you can unravel its messages. In the depth of night, we are often trying to work through our problems of the day. If we pay attention, we may discover solutions we would not normally have encountered.

- Keep a journal or paper and pen next to your bed. Try documenting your dreams upon awakening for a week or so.

- Tell yourself before drifting off to sleep that you'll be able to recall any relevant information from a dream.

- When stuck on a problem or with a situation you can't seem to resolve, ask for answers to be given to you during your dreaming time.

- When you find yourself daydreaming, don't dismiss any thoughts of a future your daydream creates. Write it down, and commit to making it concrete if it feels right.

Many books, dreams, and dream journals later, I'm still intrigued with the power of dreams.

> All human beings are also dream beings. Dreaming ties all mankind together.
>
> —JACK KEROUAC,
> *On the Road*

chapter forty-six

Watch Your Garden Grow

I 'd like to suggest that your garden can be a garden in the traditional sense—one with flowers, shrubs, veggies, and herbs—or it can be a garden of delights in your mind. What ideas are you nurturing? What seeds of hope have you planted lately? As you watch your garden grow, keep in mind that your thoughts are like seeds. As one of my cards states, "Sow your seeds... Voice your vision... All comes to fruition!"

To be honest, I'm not the greatest gardener in the world. Even though I can be proud of growing flowers, tomatoes, and lavender in my backyard when I lived in Seattle, I really wasn't born with a green thumb. That would be my sister, Beth, who can spend hours and hours tending to her acreage where she lives in the Upper Peninsula of Michigan. I'm amazed when I read an email of all the work she accomplishes in one day. She should be the one who writes this chapter, I realize, because she has real, practical experience in growing a large garden—she knows the intricacies of what to plant, when to plant, how to prepare the soil. She grows so much food that she has plenty of her bounty to freeze, can, and share. She and Randy, her husband, make salsa and spaghetti sauce from the tomatoes, and press and make apple cider from their apple trees. I checked in with her recently and she told me they are about to harvest beans, corn, and squash, plus onions, garlic, lettuce, spinach, radishes, carrots, and beets.

She's already frozen asparagus, strawberries, and blueberries. I'm in awe.

Beth said that she loves having fresh flowers available for cutting. As with most things, some years are better than others for growing flowers. This year she had a ton of aphids on her heliopsis in front of her house, but none on the ones by the veggie garden. The butterfly bush isn't doing too great this year, but the spirea bush went nuts. She reports that her lavender is spreading like wildfire and she'll have to transplant half of it next spring. Her roses are doing great this year, but last year wasn't good for them.

Where we live now, in the upstairs flat of a Victorian house in San Francisco, we have back steps that lead down to a small city-sized backyard that is not conducive to plants or a garden. The first summer we lived here I attempted to plant both flowers and veggies, neither of which did very well in the poor soil and with my less-than-green thumb. Even though I prepared the ground, digging out the gravel (a previous tenant, a roofer, dumped loads of gravel in the back), and adding in new dirt, mulch, and fertilizer, the loving care I extended toward the plants did not translate into bountiful produce or blooms. I pretty much gave up and decided to become an urban gardener, growing plants in containers instead—so my steps and tiny deck are now filled with terra-cotta pots of varying sizes. I've discovered the best plants for me are succulents! They are easy to maintain, they thrive despite my neglect, and they look good all the time.

I think what I like most about gardening is that it can be a metaphor for living life. Just like the roses that are doing well this year for Beth but didn't do so well last year, we have good times and not so good times. It's important to weed your garden just as you weed out the negative thoughts, fears, and doubts in your mind. The rhythm of life shows up in the garden just as it does in other aspects of your life. When we learn to dance with the seasons and play with the creativity of Mother Nature, we can really enjoy the bounty and the joy of life as expressed in a beautiful garden.

What magic do you perform when playing in the dirt? How do you create with Mother Nature? I love to translate the beauty of the garden to my watercolors. Others capture the bounty of the garden as they prepare food. Some take copious notes on the plantings and write with eloquence about their garden. No matter how you approach it, a garden is ripe with ways to record and savor its glorious offerings.

- Get out and dig in the dirt!
- Write about it.
- Draw, sketch, or do a painting of your garden's blooms.
- Cook up a meal from your veggies and record the process.

The glory of gardening: hands in the dirt, head in the sun, heart with nature. To nurture a garden is to feed not just the body, but the soul.

—ALFRED AUSTIN,
English poet laureate, 1896

chapter forty-seven

Dive into the Unknown

During the fall when I was preparing to leave Seattle and move to San Francisco, I found myself telling family, friends, clients, and coworkers that I felt like I was about to "dive into the unknown." The image that always came to me was someone diving from a tall cliff into a dark pool of water. I had *no* idea what my life was going to look like. It didn't make any sense to me, yet there was some intrigue that kept me moving forward. With this move, I was giving up so much: a home of 19 years that I loved (to move to an apartment in a not-so-great neighborhood of San Francisco); a job that I enjoyed (as a rep for a commercial carpet manufacturer); my kids (both young adults who had already left the nest); my friends (after 20 years of living in Seattle I had amassed many good friends). And all for what? The unknown? Was I crazy?

And yet it was the dive into the unknown that allowed for my deeper desire to live this creative life to bubble up to the surface. "I had to give up so much of who I was in order to become what I am now." As I mentioned before, I paired those words with a butterfly image for one of my greeting cards. Inside the card it says: "Fly free!"

I think, today, we are all being challenged to dive into the unknown. The economy, after six years of sluggish recovery, is still sputtering along, and people are apprehensive about the

185

future. We are facing the unknown as we look into the face of climate change. You can't deny the fact that weather patterns have changed and extremes are becoming the norm, be it hurricanes, winter storms, flash floods, or average daily temperatures. Mother Nature is responding to climate change, no doubt. The baby boom generation marches into advanced age with the unknown of how society will cope with the bubble of an entire generation requiring increased healthcare and services for the elderly.

I think the best answer to all this uncertainty is to focus on showing up in the world as the authentic person that you are in your heart. Live your brilliance! Share your gifts with the world. Do what you can to make your life the best it can be and take the risk, when you are called, to dive deep into the pool. You'll resurface with a completely new vision of what's possible.

- What is calling you to dive into the unknown?

- Scary as the unknown is, be open to the joy and adventure that will unfold as wings are given to you to lift you to new heights!

- Be open to floating for a period of time. The answers are not always immediate, but trust that they will arrive.

Understand that it will be difficult some days, but know that the benefits of being yourself far outweigh the pain of leaving behind much of what you know and are comfortable with. And don't think you've got to pack up and move 700 miles away, as I did. Your "unknown" will most likely show up in a way that will be unique for you.

Recall the story from chapter 1: You've got to make the jump first before the wings begin to unfurl! Fly Free!

Never be afraid to trust an unknown future
to a known God.

—CORRIE TEN BOOM,
The Hiding Place

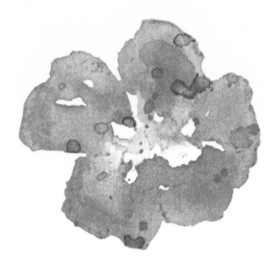

chapter forty-eight

Be in Balance

It's the Autumn Equinox today, as I write, when the hours of light are equal to the hours of darkness. In other words, day is in perfect balance with night. This is also the day when the sun moves into the sign of Libra, appropriately enough with its symbol of the golden scales, everything in balance. Being born under the sign of Libra, I'm constantly striving to maintain a balance in life. When I worked in the corporate world, I was constantly advocating a work/life balance not only for myself, but for those I worked with and for as well. I would often point out the benefits of a balanced lifestyle, suggesting that it just wasn't healthy to be all work and no play. I never understood how someone could work so many hours that they would forgo a balance that allowed for recreation, socializing, and experiencing the fullness of life. I couldn't do it. A balanced lifestyle is critical to my peace of mind.

I have learned that it is when I'm out of balance that I'm most likely to become upset or disturbed, act irrationally, do something stupid, or misinterpret what someone is trying to tell me. Life is precarious. It's so easy to be tipped one way or the other, like a seesaw at the playground. When you jump on with someone who is heavier than you—woop! Up you go. In order to keep the seesaw level, your weight needs to be balanced. I realized years ago that balance for me means equal time between being and doing. My seesaw had "being" on one seat and "doing" on the other. If there was too much doing (taking care of kids and other people, working too much at the office, keeping up with the daily chores of living), and not enough being (time for myself: nap time, journal writing time, creative time)—woop! Up went one side. It would take a while to bring the seesaw horizontal, back in balance, as I worked on the being/doing equation.

I also became aware, years ago, that I am both an introvert and an extrovert. Again, I needed to strike a healthy balance between the two. My extroverted sales personality thrived on meeting new people, working in a team, and interacting with clients, installers, support staff, and others I came in contact with for my job. Yet I discovered that in order to be at my optimum level, I needed to balance my outgoing personality with the introvert who is restored by sitting quietly, writing in a journal, reading a book, or playing with my paints. I think the introvert/extravert balance is similar in many ways to the being/doing balance. When I'm in balance, I find that life flows effortlessly; synchronicity and coincidences are the norm rather than the exception.

I was out walking along Heron's Head Park in San Francisco with my trusted and true friend Lauren. She was telling me how she had stayed inside all day the day before, confronted with computer issues that she was not able to solve. It was a frustrating day. The contrast between technology and nature was very apparent as we walked along: the gentle waves lapping the shore providing background music, the birds soaring overhead, the warmth of the sun enveloping us. She recognized the importance of regularly getting out into nature—it nourished her. She realized that the technology that is her business needs to be balanced with time spent outdoors. So she committed to taking a two-mile walk each week to one of her favorite spots in the Bay Area. It's safe to say that her seesaw has technology on one seat and nature on the other. Finding that balance will help her maintain her equilibrium when it comes to working with computers and designing websites.

Everything in moderation, I'm fond of saying. I want to walk the middle path, not too far to the right or the left. Everything in equal measure.

- What do you do to maintain a healthy, balanced lifestyle?
- What sits on your seesaw? How do you balance it?
- How do you walk the middle path?
- Explore the being/doing equation. Does being conscious of the equation help you maintain it?

My point is, life is about balance. The good and the bad. The highs and the lows. The piña and the colada.

—ELLEN DEGENERES,
Seriously...I'm Kidding

chapter forty-nine

Allow Life to Unfold

"As the blossom opens to reveal the beauty of the flower... So does each day dawn... Filled with inherent gifts and moments." So read the words to one of my inspirational cards. I paired the words with a watercolor of my favorite flower, a purple bearded iris in the midst of unfolding. It was a perfect match and truly speaks to the inherent gifts and special moments that seem to spontaneously happen as we allow life to unfold.

One of my lifelong dilemmas is knowing how much to push life and how much to allow life to happen. My goal-focused, no-nonsense, just-do-it persona wants to figure it out, get it done, make it happen—and yet another part of me recognizes the beauty that can result when you allow life to unfold at its own pace. Instead of feeling like I need to shove boulders uphill to make whatever it is I want to see materialize, I try to allow the grace of time to reveal the beauty in the unfolding nature of life. When I do, I'm always surprised with the results: they are always far better than I could have envisioned. Trust life—it knows better than we do!

Can you think of a time when you tried so hard to make something happen and then, after untold frustrations, you just gave up? Did you then have the experience of finding what was once so elusive drop into your lap almost without any effort? How does that happen? And why? I don't have the answers, but

I do know that if I can "live the question"—as I've recently been attempting to do in certain situations where I want answers *now* but they aren't forthcoming—I will have an answer when the time is right. And it will be a far better answer than one my little mind could conceive.

Sometimes life does seem to flow effortlessly. When it unfolds just as you want it to, give thanks and praise! Be grateful, and continue to see how serendipity conspires to introduce you to the people you need to meet and places the information you need seemingly at hand. This happened to an acquaintance I made recently.

I met Gina at the Diablo Valley Quilters Guild show. I was there as a vendor, selling my greeting cards, boxed notes, and wrapping paper and showcasing my first collection of quilting fabric, which had just been made available to retail stores. All the women who came by my booth loved the quilting fabric and wanted to know where they could purchase it. I wasn't selling the fabric to the stores, because I was the designer; Clothworks, the manufacturer, was the company that was selling the fabric. They knew the stores and it was their reps who called on the retailers. Being new to the quilting world, I didn't even know the names of the quilt stores in the area, so I kept asking, "Where do you shop?" and "What store would you like to carry the fabric?" I kept hearing the name "Wooden Gate," a store in Danville, and also heard that it was for sale. Then I heard that someone had purchased it. The following day, Sunday, Gina came up and introduced herself as the new owner of the Wooden Gate. So many had told her about my fabric that she wanted to come see for herself, she explained. We had a spirited discussion in which she told me how easily this opportunity came together for her. It was the answer to a lifelong dream.

She told me how it all seemed meant to be, from the way her mother told her about the opportunity, to the financing and availability. It was as if all the pieces of a puzzle called "How to own a quilting fabric store" just fell into place one day. Even more surprising, as we stood and talked, we discovered we were both going to be first-time attendees at the Quilt Market in Houston: I was going as a vendor and Gina was going as a retailer. I had yet to book my flight and hotel, but Gina had already booked a large suite, since she and a friend planned to attend together. She mentioned that something had come up for her friend, who was probably not going to be able to make the trip. She contacted me later that week to confirm that the room was available. Being able to share the cost of the hotel would help us both with expenses, plus we'd have someone to hang out with in the evenings. Life unfolding in all of its mysterious and glorious ways!

- Be open to life unfolding in ways unexpected.
- Watch how synchronicity happens, and when it does, allow it to unfold.
- View your life as a large 1,000-piece puzzle and imagine all the pieces fitting together effortlessly.

Whether or not it is clear to you, no doubt the Universe is unfolding as it should.

—MAX EHRMANN,
author of the poem "Desiderata"

chapter fifty

Look beyond the Obvious

I was in Florida on vacation, and my husband and I were sitting at an outdoor restaurant enjoying late-afternoon appetizers and glasses of wine. I had brought my travel watercolors with me, intent on playing with my paints, hoping to capture the essence of the scenic view of surf, sand, and sea which stretched out before us. The palms were blowing in the wind, providing a possible subject matter, but I thought, Do I really need more paintings of palm trees? Then, looking the other direction across the parking lot, I spotted some blue-and-white striped awnings shading the windows of a terra-cotta stucco building. I loved the intense color and strong design of the image. It was just waiting to be captured by my watercolors!

After I finished the painting, I marveled at how different it looked from what I had expected to record. No beach scene in this watercolor. Instead of colorful palms waving in the wind over a turquoise ocean, I had painted a deep-ochre-colored wall punctuated with blue-and-white striped awnings over windows. That painting came about simply because I turned my head to look in a different direction.

I thought about this last week in my yoga class. We began, as we often do, in headstand position. It took me a while to master, but I'm happy to say I can do a headstand. As I was standing on my head looking at the opposite side of the room upside down,

I thought to myself, now here's another way to look beyond the obvious! Not that most people are going to invert themselves into a headstand position just to get a different view of the world, but it did make me consider that we can look at things from a number of angles, positions, and viewpoints. When we take the time to look beyond the normal way of seeing, more is revealed to us. That's when the real fun begins, because you have the opportunity to contemplate a different response. Or the new vision allows for a new understanding of your problem or relationship, providing the insight needed to make the change you've been feeling you need to make. You will have an "aha!" moment as you suddenly see what wasn't in your field of vision until you looked beyond the obvious.

- Look beyond what you think the answer might be. Once you engage a different perspective, you typically see a different solution. Look at the world differently!

- Play with this idea by thinking of something and then physically turning yourself around. Think about it again. Look at it from a different perspective. How does it change when you change your viewpoint?

- Record your insights so you can recall them when needed.

- Engage the process when you feel stuck and not sure what to do.

That's the way things come clear. All of a sudden. And
then you realize how obvious they've been all along.

—MADELEINE L'ENGLE,
A Wrinkle in Time

chapter fifty-one
Wake Up with the Sun

B enjamin Franklin knew what he was talking about when he wrote these words: "Early to bed and early to rise, makes a man healthy, wealthy, and wise." By waking up with the sun, Franklin was encouraging readers of his *Poor Richard's Almanac* to be productive with their time: to take advantage of the early-morning hours.

What can early rising do for you? It allows you to find a few precious moments of quiet time to meditate. Or watch the splendor of a morning sunrise as it splashes the sky with a riot of colors. You can listen to the birds chirp, walk in the grass barefoot on a summer morning, or witness the calm, placid waters of the lake outside your cabin door while on a vacation. And when you get a jump on your day, you add extra hours to a life well lived.

My husband and I like to head out about 6:30 a.m. on our bikes, just as the light is taking over from the night. Everything appears so peaceful at this hour. The activity of the day has yet to take over. The streets are nearly empty. No rumbling trucks or honking cars or scores of people scurrying about. The energy is subdued in the city, and yet we are energized as we pedal along the waterfront, around the ballpark, down the Embarcadero to Fisherman's Wharf, and back home. We soak up the stillness and beauty of a day on the verge of bursting wide open into its fullness. Being out and enjoying a bike ride at sunrise sets the tone for the remainder of our day.

When the morning sun is rising later each day, as time marches on toward the Winter Solstice and the darkest day of the year, it's dark when I begin walking at about 6:00 am. But it doesn't take long for the eastern sky to lighten and dawn to break. By the time I cross the Islais Creek Bridge, gazing east over the San Francisco Bay, the sun just peeks over the horizon, casting its reflection into one long line in the water. I am captivated by the image and record it on my phone's camera. The sunrise has begun. The day is set in motion and I am filled with the splendor of it.

Besides greeting the day with equanimity and stillness, there are many other benefits to rising early:

- Having the time to eat breakfast, the most important meal of the day. It breaks our fast and fuels our body for the tasks ahead.

- Taking time to indulge in yourself. Uninterrupted time to meditate or exercise or work on your creative projects before heading out to begin your normal day satisfies and feeds the soul.

- Allowing for the time needed to organize your day, so you can work the day rather than the day working you.

- After trying it for some time, note what you enjoy most about rising early. Is it a practice you will continue?

When you rise in the morning, give thanks for the light, for your life, for your strength. Give thanks for your food and for the joy of living. If you see no reason to give thanks, the fault lies in yourself.

—TECUMSEH,
Native American leader of the Shawnee

chapter fifty-two
Lean into Life

L ean into Life": a fitting directive for the last chapter of a book filled with anecdotes, bullet points, and questions to encourage you to live a life you've always imagined.

I thought of this phrase as I leaned into the steep uphill of a sidewalk in my neighborhood, taking baby steps in order to manage the incline. I thought, How appropriate. This need to lean in, to take small steps toward your goals, to make progress uphill till the summit is reached, is taking life on your terms. Living it the way you imagine it, with ease, grace, and balance. We are always expanding, exploring, and experiencing what life has to offer with its rich kaleidoscope of opportunities, surprises, and challenges.

As I reflected on how to integrate all the information proposed in these chapters, I had the experience of living in moments filled with magic and miracles. Serendipities and synchronicities became the order of the day.

It began as I was headed down to pick up a large canvas reproduction of one of my watercolors. That in itself is a miracle. A woman contacted me after she received one of my greeting cards and fell in love with the image. She told me she had been looking for 10 years for a piece of art to hang in her bedroom. My artwork was what she wanted. She asked if I could make a larger reproduction of it. I was flabbergasted that the image on a 5 x 7 greeting card was the answer to her 10-year search for a piece of art!

We began a dialogue that led to meeting face-to-face. I was so touched by Olga's love of my blue hydrangea painting, and seeing this as an opportunity to see my art expand to wall art, I said yes, I would research the steps needed to reproduce the image on a 42 x 42 stretched canvas. I knew that the company that does my high-resolution scans also prints artwork on canvas and archival paper for artists. I asked questions, got a quote, and put together a proposal for Olga. She accepted it.

When my stretched canvas artwork was ready, I decided to pick it up on my way to pick up my friend Michaela. We were headed for the ocean to do a blessing ritual for the completion of this book. As I was maneuvering the large canvas into the back of the car, I had the exciting idea of taking a photograph of it outdoors with the ocean as the backdrop. I wanted a picture of myself with the painting before I had to give it away—what better place than Ocean Beach at sunset!

Michaela asked to make a quick stop for her, so I parked as she ran into a coffee shop. I saw a guy walking his dog, looked closer, and recognized my friend Steve. I jumped out of the car, yelling his name. How fun to see him—we'd been trading emails trying to set a date for lunch. I began to realize how the day seemed to be unfolding with all sorts of surprises; more were to follow. Michaela returned to the car and asked if we could pick up Karla, another friend. Off we went down Fulton Street headed to Karla's and then Ocean Beach.

As I parked the car and we began to unload, I noticed we were being serenaded with drumming. Three guys were drumming away with bongos, congas, and a snare set on the sidewalk. I love the sound of drums—I thanked the gods for this lovely music filling the air! We set up the photo shoot for the canvas right there on the sidewalk. After that was complete, we returned the canvas to the car and headed down to the beach for our book-blessing ritual.

The sun had set and the sky was a riot of red and orange against a backdrop of blue. Michaela, a practicing shaman, had the idea to do this blessing, and she brought the tools and instruments that she uses in ceremonies. We wrapped the book (copied pages of my chapters, placed in a three-ring binder) in a special cloth. She placed some of her ceremonial rocks on it and a few of the roses she had advised me to purchase at Safeway. Michaela explained how everything has a soul, and now that the book was written, with the exception of this last chapter, it had a life of its own. Karla referred to it as my third child. I laughed as I considered that it took a nine-month gestation period to bring it into being.

Michaela asked what my hopes for the book were. I expressed the hope that the inspiration set forth in the book would go out to the world, enriching the lives of those who read it. I talked about how one person might read the book and might convey the ideas to another. Like the ripples in a pond, the positive vibes would undulate outward, touching those who would benefit from the message. I gave thanks for all the books I've read that contributed to the knowledge I share in this book; for all the people in my life who have contributed to my being able to write this book; for all the spirit guides, angels, saints, and fairies who also contributed to this book. We talked about how the book would grow and change as it evolved through the editing process and was prepared for publication. It was a spirited discussion as the evening sky turned to night. The ocean lent its gentle sound of waves and the scent of the sea as the sky segued into a deepening darkness lit by the crescent moon, bright Venus shining next to it. We finished as the stars were popping out in the night sky, twinkling and sparkling on us. I felt blessed beyond measure for all the events that brought me to that place and time.

My hope for you, dear reader, is that you too can begin to notice the little things, see magic and miracles unfolding in your life, live in the moment, relish spontaneous surprises, have fun and play with life, create inspired activities, watch sunrises and sunsets, and enjoy life to the fullest as you create and define life on your terms!

- Hold the vision of your best life, and then live it while holding that intention.
- Lean into your life, enjoying each moment as it unfolds.
- Create, play, and explore all of life.

Live with intention. Walk to the edge. Listen Hard. Practice wellness. Play with abandon. Laugh. Choose with no regrets. Appreciate your friends. Continue to learn. Do what you love. Live as if this is all there is.

—MARY ANNE RADMACHER,
Lean Forward into Your Life

Peg Conley's love of nature has always been huge a part of her life. She grew up in Indiana and would often jump on her bike, riding out amongst the cornfields to sit by a creek and contemplate life. Since 1981, when she drove her VW bug "out west," she has lived in Salt Lake City, Seattle, and, most recently, in San Francisco—all places accessible to good hikes, beautiful gardens, and exquisite scenery.

Even while raising a family, creating a home life, and working in the corporate sales world, Peg always found time to capture nature's creations in her watercolors. The beauty of the flower, the elegance of the moon, the simplicity of bare trees, and the majesty of mountains are all sources that continually inspire her. Aside from nature, Peg also possesses a long-held fascination with words; as a child, she either had her nose in a book or a pen in her hand—a trait that earned her the title of "bookworm."

Currently living the creative life she has always imagined, Peg is grateful for the *aha!* moments that have led her to this point. She has combined her two loves—words and watercolors—into her own greeting card and gift line, and she is absolutely thrilled to add "author" to the "artist/entrepreneur" tag she now wears after the publication of her book *Imagine the Life You'd Love to Live, Then Live It.*

Peg now happily resides in San Francisco with her husband and two cats.

Peg's work can be found at her own website, www.wordsandwatercolors.com, as well as at the websites of manufacturers who have licensed her work: Clothworks (quilting fabric), CoasterStone (stone coasters), and Laila's (canvas wall art). She can also be followed on Facebook and Twitter.

to our readers

Viva Editions publishes books that inform, enlighten, and entertain. We do our best to bring you, the reader, quality books that celebrate life, inspire the mind, revive the spirit, and enhance lives all around. Our authors are practical visionaries: people who offer deep wisdom in a hopeful and helpful manner. Viva was launched with an attitude of growth and we want to spread our joy and offer our support and advice where we can to help you live the Viva way: vivaciously!

We're grateful for all our readers and want to keep bringing you books for inspired living. We invite you to write to us with your comments and suggestions, and what you'd like to see more of. You can also sign up for our online newsletter to learn about new titles, author events, and special offers.

Viva Editions
2246 Sixth St.
Berkeley, CA 94710
www.vivaeditions.com
(800) 780-2279
Follow us on Twitter @vivaeditions
Friend/fan us on Facebook